Chandra Shekhar Azad is a matchless personality of the Indian revolutionary movement. His love for the freedom of India to the exclusion of all else, indomitable courage and commendable strength of character will ideally inspire for ever the custodians of freedom of our nation. The ideal of patriotism which he, though born in a very indigent family, presented is not only commendable but adorable as well. Azad, in fact, is a symbol of virtues such as love for the country, renunciation and self sacrifice.

Chandra Shekhar Azad:

An Immortal Revolutionary of India

By

Dr. Bhavan Singh Rana

Translated by

Dr. Brij Bhushan Paliwal

Diamond Books

© Publisher

Publisher	:	**Diamond Pocket Books (P) Ltd.**
		X-30, Okhla Industrial Area, Phase-II
		New Delhi-110020
Phone	:	011-40712200
E-mail	:	sales@dpb.in
Website	:	www.dpb.in
Edition	:	2024

Chandra Shekhar Azad : An Immortal Revolutionary of India
By : Dr. Bhawan Singh Rana

Preface

The contribution of the revolutionaries in attaining freedom for India and the formation of this nation has not been less in any respect when compared to other movements. The fact is that the history of India's fight for freedom begins with the uprising of 1857. However, it is a matter of regret that our historians have not made correct evaluation of the contribution of the revolutionaries.

Chandra Shekhar Azad is a matchless personality of the Indian revolutionary movement. His love for the freedom of India to the exclusion of all else, indomitable courage and commendable strength of character will ideally inspire for ever the custodians of freedom of our nation. The ideal of patriotism which he, though born in a very indigent family, presented is not only commendable but adorable as well. Azad, in fact, is a symbol of virtues such as love for the country, renunciation and self sacrifice.

The great men of India have lived by the tradition of keeping themselves away from self praise. Likewise, Azad also never told his associates anything about himself. Once, when Bhagat Singh enquired about his home and family, he said, "Party is concerned with me, not my family. I do not want anybody to write my biography." Besides, the movements of the revolutionaries were always secret and covert. Therefore, it appears well nigh impossible to write an undisputed history of their uprisings. That is why different books give different versions of the incidents of the life of Azad.

A brief attempt has been made in this book to string together in a chronological order the material available in respect of all the incidents in Azad's life. Mention has been made at appropriate places where scholars differ regarding some incidents. Only discerning readers will decide as to how successful this attempt has been.

This book is just a collection of the historical incidents related to the life of Azad. Therefore, any claim regarding its originality will only be a delusion. I acknowledge my gratefulness to scholars like Shri Manmath Nath Gupta, Yash Pal, Vaishampayan, Shri Virendra, Vyathit Hridaya, Yash Pal Sharma, Shiv Verma, Sita Ramayya from whose books I have liberally drawn.

— Bhavan Singh Rana

Contents

1
Early Life

We hardly know the names of many of the brave sons of India who sacrificed their lives in obtaining freedom for this country and the formation of this nation. It seems that we have almost forgotten those revolutionaries also whose names we do know. Their names are limited to the books of history only. The history of India's fight for freedom begins with the uprising of 1857. Though the Britishers quelled this first fight for freedom, the Indians, who were chained in slavery, drew inspiration from it and continued to work for their independence. People and parties, after the formation of Indian National Congress, fought their war of independence through non-violent means. However, the entire credit for India's independence goes to the Congress today. Many revolutionary sons of India fought a parallel war for India's independence, against the Britishers along with the Congress. These revolutionaries posed a big challenge to the British Government. The aim of these revolutionaries was to throw the alien rulers out of the country and secure freedom for their motherland. The brave Indian revolutionaries continued to further their pious cause, though they had to face terrible difficulties. Quite often they risked their lives and gave up all loaves and fishes of life. One name among these top, immortal and brave sons of India is that of Chandra Shekhar Azad who sacrificed his life for the independence of his motherland. We are presenting here below the life-story of this brave soul:

Ancestry and the Place of His Origin

There are many illusions about the place of original residence of Azad as well as that of his ancestors. Azad's forefathers were basically the residents of Kanpur, who later on settled in Badarka village in Unnao district. That is why Azad's father Pandit Sita Ram Tiwari's childhood and the earlier years of his youth passed here. Pandit Sita Ram Tiwari married thrice. His first wife came from Maurawa, district Unnao. He had a son from this wife, who died early in life. Pandit Tiwari could not live long with this wife, and deserted her. She lived for the rest of her life with the people on her mother's side. Later on he married again. His second wife came from Sikanderapur, Unnao. She also could not live with him for long as she passed away soon. After that he married Jagrani Devi, his third wife. Jagrani Devi belonged to Chandraman Khera, Unnao. The Tiwari couple was blessed with a son in Badarka, Unnao. They named this son Sukhdev.

Birth and Childhood

After the birth of this son, Pandit Sita Ram moved to Alirajpur, an estate in central India, in search of livelihood. Later on he called his wife Jagrani Devi and son Sukhdev also there. He made the village Bhabhara of Alirajpur the place of his residence. Here Jagrani Devi gave birth to another son in 1905, nearly five or six years after Sukhdev. This child, later on, came to be known as Chandra Shekhar Azad. His parents were highly disappointed when they saw their new-born infant because the baby was unusually weak and his weight was much less than that of an average child. Earlier a few infants of the Tiwari couple had died. Therefore, the parents were always worried about the health of this child. The child, though weak, was very beautiful. He had a face round like the moon.

The financial condition of Tiwari was not good. First he got a very small job in the forest department. Once, some tribals beat him black and blue when he was on duty, and relieved him of money, clothes etc.—whatever he had on his person. After that he bought a few cows and buffaloes and brought up his family by selling their milk. In the severe drought of 1912 many of his cattle perished, and he was compelled to give up this vocation as well. He served in a government garden after that. His financial condition was pitiable. However, he always remained committed to honesty.

He did not bring home anything from this garden, however small. The following statement of Pandit Sita Ram Tiwari has been cited by Shri Vishwanath Vaishampayan in his book 'Chandra Shekhar Azad':

"I did not resort to any unfairness while serving in the government garden. Not to talk of a mango, I did not send even a *bharta* (brinjal) to the *tehsildar* free. I did not allow anybody from my family to touch anything. If she (referring to the mother of Azad) had ever taken a flower or fruit from here, I would have beheaded her. I never earned a single paisa dishonestly. To covet others' riches was a sin to me."

Pandit Sita Ram Tiwari could hardly provide milk or proper nourishment for Azad due to his poverty. There was a popular belief in that area that children should be fed the meat of a tiger so that they could be healthy, strong and brave. Therefore, tiger's meat was somehow fed to Azad. Possibly, people dry up this meat, keep it with themselves and feed children, when required. Except this, Azad remained a vegetarian all through his life. Though he was fond of hunting, he did not eat meat. However, later on he had started taking eggs under the influence of Bhagat Singh.

The lean and thin child, Chandra Shekhar Azad, began to grow like the phases of the moon. His body became healthy and strong. This led to a new hope in his parents. A new feeling of happiness spread around. Chandra Shekhar was stubborn by nature right from his childhood. Fearlessness and courage were also inalienable parts of his nature, besides being stubborn. He would see to it that he does whatever he set his heart upon. An incident related to this trait finds mention in many books detailing his childhood. He was playing once, during Deepawali festival, with matchsticks which flare light. Then suddenly an idea flashed in young Chandra Shekhar's mind. If one matchstick flashes so much flare, how intense and dazzling will the light be if all matchsticks are flashed together? He conveyed this idea to his friends playing there. His friends were all excited to see this grand flash, but none dared to strike all the matchsticks together. Every one feared that his hand would be burnt with so many matchsticks striking together. Without waiting for a second Chandra Shekhar came forward and took upon himself to do this. He struck all the matchsticks together. There was a dazzling show of light, but his hand was burnt. Azad did not care for it. He learnt it only when his friends told him that his hand was burnt. His friends asked him to put some ointment on it. But Azad, in his characteristic manner, brushed it aside, saying it did not matter that his hand was burnt, that it would get well by itself. His friends were amazed when they heard this and just stared at his face. It was in his nature to perform such courageous deeds right from his childhood, which held portents for his life to come.

Brother-Sister

Four sons were born to Azad's mother before him. Of them only Sukhdev was alive. The other three had died before Azad was born. When Azad was a student in Benares, his elder brother, Sukhdev, had become a postman some where near his village. He worked on this post for about two years. Then he suffered from pneumonia and resigned his post. He got medical treatment, but to no avail, and died in 1925. Then Azad was left as the only live child of his parents. Probably, he did not have any real sister. Azad was at large at the time of his brother's death.

Education

Living in utter penury, Pandit Sita Ram Tiwari could hardly educate his sons. Azad's education started in a school in the village. Shri Manmath Nath Gupta writes that one gentleman, Shri Manohar Lal Trivedi, who worked on a small post in the government, taught Azad and Sukhdev at their home as tutor those days. At that time Sukhdev was around thirteen-fourteen years old and Azad was eight. Quoting Shri Trivedi, he writes:-

"I used to teach Azad when he was eight, and Sukhdev when he was thirteen-fourteen years old. Azad held high ideas and love for justice from his childhood itself. Once I was teaching them, and uttered a word wrong deliberately. On this, Azad picked up the cane, which I kept with me to subdue children while teaching, and gave me two lashes.

On this Shri Tiwari rushed towards us and wanted to beat Azad, but I stopped him. On asking, Azad's reply was—'He hits me and my brother for our mistakes. Therefore, I have hit him for his mistake!'

After this, Shri Trivedi got a transfer to Nagpur Tehsil, but he continued to visit Azad at his home. Four or five years later, he was transferred again to Khattali village, near Bhabhare. Then Shri Trivedi kept Azad with him at his home and taught as Sita Ram Tiwari was not in a position to educate him. Azad lived with Shri Manohar La Trivedi for some time. After one year his sacred thread ceremony (*Yagyopaveet-sanskar*) was performed. On this occasion he went to Bhabhra with Shri Trivedi. He studied upto fourth standard in Khattali.

Shri Sita Ram Agnihotri, a resident of Kanpur, was tehsildar in Alirajpur tehsil those days and Shri Manohar Lal Trivedi had also come to Alirajpur. Once Chandra Shekhar Azad went to see him in Alirajpur and stayed with him. He requested the tehsildar to provide some job to Azad. Shri Agnihotri, tehsildar, was fairly acquainted with the financial condition and honesty of the family of Azad. So he fixed up a job for Azad in Alirajpur tehsil itself. He was fourteen years old at that time.

Azad served here for about an year. Here he got in touch with a trader who lived in Benares and had come to Alirajpur in connexion with the trade in pearls. Azad ran away with him. He did not resign his job. Possibly, Chandra Shekhar Azad caught fancy for the roaming life of the trader. He himself did not like to be tied to anything. Azad did not like to live with that man also. He came with him to Bombay and then left him. Now he faced the problem of bread and butter. Therefore, he started working at the port. Though he found a job for himself, cooking food was still a problem because he was still a very traditional Brahmin. He lived on roasted grams for a few days in the beginning so as to keep himself free from the hassles of cooking food, but later on he started eating in the *dhabas*. In the evenings he went to cinema, so that he could sleep well at night. This was a very boring life of low level. Here he could take his bath only once a week, with great difficulty. He could have lived as a coolie only if he lived here. Therefore, he decided to leave Bombay.

Prior to this, he had perhaps expressed his desire to his father to go to Benares and study Sanskrit, but he could not get the consent of his father for some unknown reason and his own helplessness. There was nobody to stop Chandra Shekhar Azad this time. He left Bombay and reached Benares straight. There he secured admission in a Sanskrit school, and made arrangements for his stay. Then he wrote a letter home in this respect.

It is undisputed that Chandra Shekhar Azad came to Benares to study Sanskrit. But there are two opinions regarding whether he was sent to Benares or came on his own. According to one opinion, he himself rushed to Benares, as has been described above. According to the second opinion, Azad's father himself sent him to Benares because Azad had no inclination to go there. It was not possible for Pandit Sita Ram Tiwari to educate his son due to his poverty, yet he considered it his duty to educate him. Then what was to be done? After a long deliberation he decided to send his son to Benares. There was no other alternative. Benares has been a centre of Sanskrit studies from ancient times. Many scholars there even today teach students Sanskrit free, as per ancient *guruku* tradition. Besides this, many persons who loved their culture arranged free boarding and lodging for students, particularly Brahmin students who studied Sanskrit in the traditional manner. This tradition lives unto this day. Occasionally, these students are assisted financially through a donation of clothes and money (*dakshina*) by religious minded people. Pandit Sita Ram Tiwari, keeping in mind these facilities and his own financial condition, sent his child, Chandra Shekhar, to Benares to study Sanskrit.

Azad felt out of sorts in the new environment, having come very far away from his home for the first time. The child in him rebelled. He ran away from there and reached Alirajpur estate, where his uncle lived. Vivacious and fearless child, Chandra Shekhar came in contact with Bhils (tribals) here. He learnt the use of bow and arrow in the company of Bhils. He became expert in hitting the target with an arrow.

Every society has its own traditions. Likewise in the Bhil society there is the practice of punishing the convict by hitting him with an arrow. Once a Bhil was being punished through an arrow for allegation of misconduct. In the meanwhile, Chandra Shekhar arrived there. According to the rules of the Bhils any one who reaches there can take an aim. Chandra Shekhar was also asked to take an aim. He was a champion hit man. His arrows hit the eyes of the guilty person. He lost vision in both the eyes. His uncle came to know of this incident. He was furious with Chandra Shekhar. He did not deem it proper that Chandra Shekhar lived in the company of the Bhils. He thought to himself that this way Chandra Shekhar would ruin his life. Resultingly, he sent Chandra Shekhar to Benares again.

This time Chandra Shekhar acted intelligently. He devoted himself to his studies, but he could not develop a taste for Sanskrit grammar as it involved a lot of cramming. However, here he studied Sanskrit language and its grammar in a general way. He lived in a *dharamshala* (a free lodging house) here. Food was also provided by the *dharamshala* management.

Chandra Shekhar was naughty by nature since childhood. He did not relish to live at a place for long. Therefore, he occasionally jumped into the Ganga and swam for hours. Sometimes he sat where a discourse on the Ramayana, the Mahabharata or the Puranas was going on and listened intently. He liked, right from his childhood, to listen to the stories of patriots and brave men.

From Student Life to Politics

When Chandra Shekhar was studying in Benares, Mahatma Gandhi had entered the political life of India. With this the activities of the revolutionaries had also begun to increase throughout India. The British Government constituted a committee to suppress the Indians. Justice A.S.T. Rowlett was the president of this committee, with the following four other members:

1. Basel Scott, Chief Justice, Bombay High Court.
2. Coomer Swami Shastri, Justice, Madras High Court.
3. Burney Lorett, member, Board of Revenue, U.P.
4. Prabhat Chandra Mitra, Advocate, Calcutta High Court.

While constituting this committee, its twin objectives were defined as: (i) To collect comprehensive informat'on about the activities of the revolutionaries in India, and (ii) to make law to suppress them.

It is clear that the aim of this committee was to suppress the voice of Indians clamouring for freedom. But the logic advanced by the Government was that the committee was constituted to bring about reforms. This committee was constituted on 10th December, 1917. The committee presented its final report of 226 pages. Indians' freedom and rights were further reduced, pursuant to this report. This report not only suppressed the agitations of the revolutionaries, its aim was to suppress political agitations also. The name of this committee was 'Sedition Committee' and, consequently, even the political agitations could be suppressed through this committee by terming them as 'rebellion'. This report was based on the views of the police. This report placed the hawkish Congressmen like Lokmanya Bal Gangadhar Tilak, Bipin Chandra Pal et al at par with revolutionaries like Chafekar brothers, Khudi Ram Bose etc. No consideration about violence or non-violence was taken into account.

Recommendations of the Rowlett Committee

This committee gave extensive rights to the police. Police could put anybody anytime under custody, house arrest, search or ask for bonds. Thus on one side the Police got draconian powers on the recommendations of this committee; on the other side, it affected the working of the courts also. It contained such recommendations also that the accused could be punished at the earliest without sufficient evidence. The government accepted these recommendations, and they were called the Rowlett Bill.

Countrywide Opposition to the Rowlett Act

A wave of discontentment swept through the country in early 1919 as soon as this report was published. The Congress opposed it calling it a body-blow to the fundamental rights of the Indians. Mahatma Gandhi warned that

Satyagraha would be launched in the whole country and asked for a countrywide strike on 30th March, 1919. Though this date was changed to 6th April, 1919, yet, in the absence of information, Delhi observed a successful strike on 30th March. A mammoth procession was taken out, led by Swami Shradhanand, the president of Arya Samaj. The white policemen threatened Swamiji to shoot him down, but Swamiji was not at all perturbed by it. He continued to advance. Police fired at Delhi railway station in which five persons were killed and twenty wounded. Countrymen's love for freedom wanted to break loose the chains of slavery. The government wanted to stamp them out. It was at its wits end and did not know what to do.

This agitation in Delhi showed Hindus and Muslims in an unprecedented show of unity. Both made this agitation successful, working shoulder to shoulder. Hindus publicly drank water from the hands of Muslims, and on 4th April, 1919 Swami Shradhanand delivered a speech from the precints of Shahi Jama Masjid, reciting *mantras* from the *Vedas*. No doubt this is a rare event of Indian history. This is one of the brightest historical chapters.

The bill was opposed in the whole country, as in Delhi. In 1919 the Congress session was to be held in Amritsar. Dr. Kichlu and Satya Pal were busy making preparations for it. The government arrested both of them and sent them to an unknown destination. The public moved on to the office of the magistrate to know why this was done, but the police stopped it on the way. In the meanwhile violent riots broke out in which five white men were killed. Fire was set in many houses. The anger of the public knew no bounds. Violent incidents took place in Gujranwala and Kasur also. Dr. Satya Pal had written to Gandhi, inviting him to come to Amritsar. Gandhi left for Punjab on 8th April. On his way, he was arrested at Palwal station and sent back to Bombay.

Processions were taken out in the whole Punjab protesting against the Rowlett Act. Processions as long as three miles were seen on the roads. Roads were packed with processionists. Black flags were demonstrated, strike was also observed along with processions. This strike continued for seven days. Police forced some shopkeepers to open their shops, but as soon as the police shifted from there, the shops were closed again. In Lahore food was cooked in lanes during strike in bazars. Women worked in the lanes as volunteers so that the public and workers, who depended on their daily wages, were fed and did not go hungry. People rose above their narrow selfish interests and participated in the agitation in the interest of their country. Everywhere people were shouting "Rowlett Act Hai Hai" (Down with the Rowlett Act). Effigies of Emperor George V were lurnt. Police lathi-charged people at various places as per its whim and fancy. At many places the police fired. Public caning of the processionists in the bazar and indiscriminate and instantaneous arrests became common features. The government pasted posters asking people to end strike and stop processions. But the public tore and removed them as soon as they were pasted.

Jalianwala Bagh Kand

On 13th April, 1919, the Baisakhi day, a meeting was in progress at the Jalianwala Bagh. The object of the meeting was to register protest against the Rowlett Act. It was attended by around twenty thousand people, including children, youths, adults, the old and men and women of all ages. Jalianwala Bagh had walls on all four sides, with only one small, narrow passage from which even a vehicle could not pass.

The meeting was peaceful. A man named Hansraj was addressing. Meanwhile General Dyer reached there. He had 50 white and a hundred Indian soldiers. He asked his soldiers to stand on one side and ordered firing on the unarmed people. People ran helter skelter but the escape route was unusually narrow. Many people jumped into the well to save their lives, but perished there. Firing continued for two-three minutes, drenching the innocent people in blood bath. It was a mad dance of violence. Shri Manmath Nath Gupta, in his book '*Bharatiya Krantikari Andolan Ka Itihas*' (The History of the Indian Revolutionary Movement) describes it—

"According to the statement which General Dyer made before the Hunter Commission, he first asked people to disperse. Then within two-three minutes he ordered firing. Even if this is accepted as the truth, then twenty thousand people could not go out in two minutes through a narrow passage. If this is assumed that the people refused to leave despite orders from General Dyer, even then it is difficult to understand as to what was the need or where was the emergency to shoot-dead a thousand people just in no time. It would be wrong to put the blame for this incident on General Dyer, because I think that the British imperialism carried these executions in according to a carefully planned strategy. The fact is that the British imperialism got the best jawans from Punjab. Therefore, naturally the government did not want any kind of disorder in this province. In this respect the government wanted to practise the policy of nipping in the bud any agitation. General Dyer saw that the firing continued till his anger cooled off. And he confessed it before the Commission with a lot of arrogance. And why should he not say, as he was not afraid of anybody."

In this massacre in all one thousand six hundred shots were fired. As per the Govt. report 400 persons died and nearly two thousand were wounded. The report of the government is usually incorrect in such cases. Obviously, this report was also wrong. Later on the Congress constituted a Commission of Enquiry to go into it. According to its report the number of the dead and the wounded was nearly double of what the government report stated.

The government did not relent in its act of cruelty even after this gruesome event. Supply of water and electricity to Amritsar was stopped. Wayfarers were beaten with canes, and then they were forced to crawl on their bellies and chests. The rates of goods in the shops were determined by the soldiers under the martial law. Hundreds of people were arrested and sent to jails.

Michael O'Dyer, the governor of Punjab, had praised General Dyer for this action. Shri Manmath Nath Gupta has described the atrocities of the military administration in the following words:

"Cruel atrocities were perpetrated in many other parts of Punjab also which make a hair-raising account. At some places even bombs were dropped. At many places a rule was declared that every Indian will salute every white man. A Hindu and a Muslim were tied together and taken out in a procession at times. The intention of the government was to mock the Hindu-Muslim unity. The incharge of Kasur got a big steel cage prepared, and one hundred fifty persons were forced to live like monkeys in public view. Colonel Johnson got a marriage party caught and caned publicly. At some places respectable persons were caned in the presence of prostitutes. Wayfarers were used as coolies. It was ordered that the school children would salute the British flag three times daily. Children were forced to pledge that they would not resort to crime, and to repent for what they had done. Forty lakh rupees of Lala Harkishan La were seized and he was deported. There are innumerable instances. How long shall I recount. . ."

The whole India was plunged into deep anguish due to incidents in Punjab. Chandra Shekhar knew all this. He read about all these incidents in the newspapers. Teen Chandra Shekhar's blood boiled on these atrocities perpetrated by the alien Britishers on his countrymen. His heart was inflammed with a fire for revenge. He was just fourteen years old at this time.

Punishment through Caning and Transformation from Chandra Shekhar to 'Azad'

After Amritsar the next session of the Congress was held in Calcutta in 1920. It was a special session and Lala Lajpat Rai was made the president. A resolution asking for non-co-operation with the government was tabled in this session. Though old leaders like Deshbandhu Chitranjan Das, Mahamana Madan Mohan Malviya, Bipin Chandra Pal et al were against it, the resolution was passed. Again in this year itself the annual session of the Congress was held in Nagpur which had Vijay Raghavacharya as its president. In this session also this resolution was passed with heavy majority.

Noncooperation movement was launched in the beginning of 1921 in the whole country under the leadership of Mahatma Gandhi. The storm of noncooperation spread through the length and breadth of the country in all its fury. Bonfires of foreign clothes were made. The advocates boycotted the courts. Students started boycotting the government schools as well as the government aided schools. The agitationists picketed the shop selling foreign goods. Meetings were organised all over. Processions were taken out. Leaders were calling upon the public not to cooperate with the government in any way.

Like the rest of the country, Benares too could not remain untouched by this movement. Many students plunged into this movement. They abandoned their studies. Demonstrations and meetings became daily routine and slogans rent the air all around. Police rained *lathis* on the public taking part in the noncooperation movement. Chandra Shekhar attended the meetings, listened to the lectures, and saw the atrocities of the police. All these things shook his teenaged heart. When he saw the atrocities of the police, his heart rebelled. He was a lover of freedom from the very beginning. Therefore, he could not control himself. Leaving his studies behind, he jumped into the fray of the noncooperation movement. He was just around fifteen years of age at that time.

One day some agitationists were picketing a shop of foreign clothes. In the meanwhile the police arrived. One sub-inspector of police started raining blows on picketers. He was beating them black and blue. Chandra Shekhar could not bear this atrocity. He could not control himself. A stone was lying nearby. He threw that stone from a distance, aiming at the head of the sub-inspector. The aim hit the target. It burst open the head of the sub-inspector and he fell on the ground. Another policeman saw Chandra Shekhar doing this, Chandra Shekhar also knew this. Therefore, he ran away from there, dodging the eyes of the policeman. A policeman tried to catch him, but he ran out of his bounds.

Chandra Shekhar was wearing a sandal mark on his forehead. The policeman, who saw him hitting with a stone, had identified him. Therefore, he moved out with other policemen to search him out. Search was carried out in *dharamshalas*, schools and other places where he was expected to be found. Finally, the policemen reached that *dharamshala* also where he lived. A policeman entered his room. He saw the pictures of Lala Lajpat Rai, Lokmanya Tilak, Mahatma Gandhi and other national leaders. Chandra

Shekhar was arrested. He was handcuffed. The policemen took him with them, but Chandra Shekhar was not in the least afraid of it or was perturbed.

He was put in the lock-up after being taken to the police Station. Many *satyagrahis* (persons who insisted upon and stood for the truth) were imprisoned there and packed in very small rooms like animals. Proper arrangement for water or air was not there. No bedding or any other cloth to cover was provided to Chandra Shekhar in the lockup. Possibly the policemen thought that the boy would be terrified at the prospect of cold night and beg to be excused. But nothing of the sort happened. A sub-inspector of police came near his room at midnight to see what the boy was doing. Possibly he was thinking to himself that Chandra Shekhar would be shivering with cold. The sub-inspector opened the lock and went in to see. But he was surprised to see Chandra Shekhar. Chandra Shekhar had found a way out to deal with the cold. He was exercising, doing dips and sit-ups. Consequently, instead of shivering in the cold, sweat was dripping from his body. The sub-inspector could hardly believe his eyes, but the reality was there for him to see. Chandra Shekhar had proved and demonstrated that no suffering could stand in the face of right strategy and hard work. The sub-inspector went back.

The next day Chandra Shekhar was produced before a magistrate in the court. Some other boys of his age were also arrested. They were also brought to the court. The magistrate, Mr. Khareghat, was a Parsee. He dealt with the political matters of Benares, but in order to play down the importance of political detainees, they were punished under section 107 for obstructing traffic on the road. Mr. Khareghat was notorious for awarding severe punishment. Chandra Shekhar was the youngest among the students. Some Sanskrit students, who studied this subject with religious inclination, were in the age group of 30-35 years. The accused usually trembled before this magistrate, but all these students stood fearless. The magistrate asked a boy standing before Chandra Shekhar: "Your name?"

"November", the boy replied.

"Your father's name?"

"December."

Mr. Khareghat considered these replies as derogatory to him. After this he asked Chandra Shekhar. "Your name?"

"Azad". Chandra Shekhar said.

"Father's name?"

"Independent."

"Where do you live?"

"In Jail."

There replies nonplussed the magistrate. Even hardened criminals dared not to reply in his presence. Therefore, boiling with anger, he sentenced Azad to fifteen severe lashes by cane. The punishment by caning was, in reality, considered severe. The accused trembled the moment they heard this punishment. Cane lashes tore through the skin of the flogged person. But Chandra Shekhar did not care for this punishment.

The Jailor of Benares, Sardar Ganda Singh, was a man of very cruel nature. He did not know anything known as mercy. He actually relished the award of punishment to the prisoners and the accused. He reached the limits of cruelty in his work. Chandra Shekhar was tied to a wooden plank to receive the lashes. He did not have any clothes except a vest on his body, because all the clothes were taken off before flogging. Before flogging the body was besmeared with a paste so that the skin did not peel off with the lashes. Ganda Singh was delighted in his heart as he was going to set the minds of the boys right. He ordered the man to start caning. Cane lashes came thick and fast. But with every cane lash Chandra Shekhar shouted back *"Mahatma Gandhi Ki Jai"* (Hail! Mahatma Gandhi). Cane lashes bloodied his entire body, but Chandra Shekhar did not utter '*Oh*'. There was no trace of suffering or anxiety on his face. All the persons, present there, were awestuck by his patience, courage and love for the country. The news of Chandra Shekhar's cane punishment spread through the whole Benares city. The public reached the jail gate to welcome him with garlands of flowers. Children, youths and the old men and women—all in the public welcomed him with garlands and flowers. They lifted him up on their shoulders, and the sky reverberated with the slogans—'*Chandra Shekhar Azad Ki Jai*', '*Bharat-Mata Ki Jai*', '*Mahatma Gandhi Ki Jai*'.

A meeting was organised at a place known as Gyan Vapi in Benares. Here a large crowd of people turned up to see, have a '*darshan*' of this brave child. When Azad appeared on the dais, flowers rained on him. He was flooded with flowers. He was wearing a *dhoti* and *kurta* on this occasion. He had a sandal '*tilak*' on his forehead. On the stage, he made a brief speech in which he prayed for working for the freedom of India and paid his tribute to the brave men who had sacrificed their lives doing this pious work. The crowd cheered again, shouting '*Chandra Shekhar Azad Zindabad*' (Long Live Chandra Shekhar Azad). After this other persons also addressed the public, in which they praised the heroic deeds of Chandra Shekhar Azad.

In those days a newspaper, Maryada, was regularly published from Benares. Its publisher was Shri Shiv Prasad Gupta, and editor Shri Sampurnanand. Shri Sampurnanand later on became the Chief Minister of Uttar Pradesh, and after that the Governor of Rajasthan. He published a photo of Chandra Shekhar Azad and an article captioned '*Brave Child Azad*', in which he profusely praised his heroic deeds and exceptional courage.

Though the magistrate, Mr. Khareghat, had sentenced Chandra Shekhar to be caned in order to teach him a lesson, this punishment further strengthened Azad's love for the motherland. In this context, Shri Manmath Nath Gupta writes in his book, *The History of Indian Revolutionary Movement*:

"Azad had challenged the magistrate. Azad had rightly said that jail was the only place for the free people to live under an alien and bad government. Mr. Khareghat had thought that he was a child and therefore he should be awarded such a punishment that he gave up all other things and concentrated on his studies. Thus, he was sentenced to fifteen cane lashes. He was taken to jail and caned. But on every succeeding cane lash, he said all the louder '*Mahatma Gandhi Ki Jai*', Those days the slogan '*Mahatma Gandhi Ki Jai*' was a slogan to India's determined march to freedom."

In fact, freedom is not so much a matter of body as that

of the spirit. A man's body can be captivated, not his spirit. A true lover of freedom becomes an eyesore to an atrocious administration. Therefore, most of their lives are spent behind the prison bars. During the British administration all the lovers of the country, the patriots, had made jail their home. Therefore, when the magistrate asked Chandra Shekhar about his home, he said it was jail. His reply carried a deep, inherent meaning which pointed towards the atrocities of the government.

This incident established Chandra Shekhar as a popular leader at an adolescent age. Though it was certainly a cruel punishment, it could be termed as very severe. It was a stepping stone to his future revolutionary life. From this point of view it was an important event. After this Chandra Shekhar became Chandra Shekhar Azad—Brave Chandra Shekhar Azad.

The news of the cane-punishment reached his home as well, since the news was reported by all the newspapers of the country. People in his family were seriously worried on reading this news. Father Shri Sita Ram Tiwari straightway dashed to Benares. He reasoned with his son in innumerable ways and advised him to return home, but Azad was very strong-willed right from childhood. He had taken a vow to serve the country. For any first rate person his aim in life is the highest thing. When a great man sets his heart upon something, he does not deviate from his path even in the face of difficulties from all over the world. Therefore, he did not acquiesce into the suggestion by his father. His father went back disappointed.

This was in a way his rebellion against his family. In fact, the whole country was his home, in the eyes of Azad. Acharya Chanakya has advised that a man should be sacrificed in the interest of the family, a family in the interest of the village, and a village should be abandoned in the interest of a country or state. Chandra Shekhar Azad did the same. He sacrificed the narrow familial affections in the interest of his motherland—India.

2
In the Direction of Revolution

After the incident described above, Chandra Shekhar Azad continued to move towards the freedom movement. He was completely imbued in patriotism. He gave up his studies, and he began to prepare his school friends to join the freedom struggle. The main aim of Azad became the attainment of independence.

Suspension of Movement: Azad's Disappointment

The noncooperation movement had pointed to a new direction to Azad, and he started dreaming of India's independence. He had some ambitions of his own in this respect, but the next year itself Mahatma Gandhi, after the incident at Chauri Chaura, suspended the noncooperation movement. It happened like this: Noncooperation movement was at its peak. Many agitationists were arrested and sent to jails. This movement was totally nonviolent. At a place named Chauri Chaura, near Gorakhpur, the agitationists lost their senses in the face of the police atrocities, and the crowd set a police station ablaze. One sub-inspector and twenty one policemen were burnt to death in this fire. This incident took place on 20th Feb., 1922, which is known as the Chauri Chaura episode in history. On seeing the incident of this nature, Gandhiji stopped the movement. On 13th March, 1922, Gandhiji was arrested. The enthusiasm of the Indians was at its highest at this time. Therefore, they were greatly disappointed by this decision of Gandhiji. About this decision of the Mahatma, Shri Manmath Nath Gupta writes—

"Mahatma Gandhi suspended the movement realising the lack of feeling of nonviolence in the common man. On

13th March, Gandhiji was also arrested. One thing in this surprises me that when the movement was going on in full steam and Gandhiji was publicly leading it, no one caught him, but as soon as the movement was suspended, the government arrested him. This was not a chance incident, because when Gandhiji was leading this movement, he was thirty three crore people, but when he suspended the movement and dashed the rising enthusiasm of the people and disappointed them due to one misconception, he became one person only."

There might be some exaggeration in these words of Shri Gupta, but one thing is certain that the Indians, particularly the youths, were highly disappointed at the suspension of the movement just for a small incident. Shri Gupta himself was a revolutionary, therefore his words reflected the true feelings of the revolutionaries of that time. Chandra Shekhar was deeply disappointed on seeing the movement suspended half way in this manner. But his disappointment was just a momentary surge, not permanent. There was no going back from the path on which he had taken decisive steps.

In Contact with the Revolutionaries

Chandra Shekhar's intense interest and active participation in the movement hampered his studies. But he got rid of them. After giving up his studies he started looking for the right environment for his work.

The revolutionary youth of India had challenged the government many times with their activities prior to the non-co-operation movement also. Benares was not untouched by these activities. The role of the Bengali revolutionaries had been important in these activities. For some time it seemed that the revolutionary movement had come to an end. The leader of the Benares Conspiracy, Shachindranath Sanyal, was deposited for life for his role in the conspiracy, and many others were also sentenced as punishment in many forms. In 1920 all political prisoners were granted amnesty. As a result, all the revolutionaries were released. Hitherto, the youth felt frustrated on account of midway stoppage of the non-co-operation movement. Shachindranath Sanyal took advantage of this situation and reorganised the revolutionary group. The main area of Sanyal was Uttar Pradesh. Very soon he developed the revolutionary group strong. In these days *Anusheelan Samiti*, an outfit of the revolutionaries, was also active. *Anusheelan Samiti* established an *ashram* (abode) in Benares, namely *Kalyan Ashram*. In fact this *ashram* was an office of the revolutionary members of the *Samiti*.

The revolutionary group and *Anusheelan Samiti* continued to run their separate activities for a long time. The aims and working practices of both were common. Therefore, later on both of them combined and started working as a group. This joint group was named 'Hindustan Republican Association.' Following were the main aims of this association:

1. To establish a democratic republic through organised revolution, in which provinces will have complete freedom in internal matters.

2. To confer the right to vote to every adult citizen, having a sane mind.

3. To establish a society free from exploitation.

It is clear that all of these aims were influenced by the system of administration in Communist Russia. Just a few years back in 1917, Communism had been adopted and established in the Soviet Union. The entire Uttar Pradesh had members of 'Hindustan Republican Association'. Pandit Ram Prasad Bismil in Shahjahanpur, Suresh Bapu in Kanpur, and Shri Rajendra Nath Lahiri, Shri Shachindra Nath Bakshi, and Ravindra Mohan Kar in Benares were active and advancing the cause of this party.

By now Chandra Shekhar Azad was a known name in Benares. So Pranavesh, a member of the revolutionary party, met him. Pranavesh was highly impressed by Azad. Thus Azad also became a member of 'Hindustan Republican Association'. Here he met great revolutionaries like Ram Prasad Bismil, and from here started a new chapter of a future revolutionary in his life.

Organising the Party

When Azad became a member of 'Hindustan Republican

Association', it was decided that the membership of the party be increased. Azad played an active role in this work. He roamed here and there in the dress of a Brahmin, met young people and knew their views. He identified the youths with revolutionary ideas and made them members of his party. In this way the membership of the party shot up due to diligent work of Azad. However, the party suffered from paucity of funds. Though manpower of the party increased heavily, but it was short of finances. Members held sittings to overcome this problem.

'*Kalyan Ashram*', referred to above, was in a way a place in Benares which these revolutionaries used as a centre for their deliberations. Here in one room many varieties of musical instruments were placed. In the evening some people engaged themselves in singing and playing musical instruments. Along with, the revolutionaries carried on their sitting and discussions in the inside room. People formed the impression that *Kalyan Ashram* was some religious organisation where some persons devote themselves to *bha an-kirtan* (devotional songs and hymns). But the reality was something else. Here the members discussed the financial position of the party also. One day the discussion was going on the topic of financial condition of the party. Chandra Shekhar was also present in the meeting. One member of the party was Ram Krishna Khatri, who was a *Sadhu* (wandering saint) of *Udaseen Sampradaya* (a sect). He presented a new plan. The plan was this: There was a *math* (religious seat) of *nirmaley sadhus* in Ghazipur. The *mahant* (religious head of the seat) of the *math* had limitless wealth, and the *math* its own large property. The *mahant* was aging and sick. It seemed that he would soon pass away. It was required that one member of the revolutionary party became his disciple, so that after the death of the *mahant* the property of the *math* and *mahant* could legitimately be used by the revolutionaries. The *mahant* needed a disciple at this time. All the members of the party considered Chandra Shekhar Azad as the most appropriate person for this work. They were fully confident that once the *mahant* saw him, he would immediately accept him as his disciple. All the members proposed with one voice the name of Chandra Shekhar for this work. But Chandra Shekhar did not agree.

He considered it hypocrisy and fraud. But seeing that the party needed money badly, Chandra Shekhar accepted it in deference to the pressure of his friends.

In the Role of a Disciple of a Mahant

Putting a comprehensive plan in place, Azad reached the above *math* in Ghazipur in the guise of a *Brahmachari Sadhu* (a celibate saint). Sandal mark on his forehead, light pink cloak, a string of *rudraksha* beads round his neck—all this was bestowing a unique grace to Azad's personality. Otherwise also his body was well proportioned, beautiful and attractive. In his personal life he was a *Brahmachari* (celibate). On reaching the *mahant* he expressed his desire to become his disciple. Seeing his attractive personality and strong body, the *mahant* immediately agreed. He became the disciple of the *mahant*. The *mahant*, in response to his service, gradually started recovering.

Nirmal Sadhus are Sikhs who worship 'Guru Granth Sahib'. Here Azad studied the *Gurmukhi* script and Punjabi language also, because these were the essential conditions to become the *mahant*.

Though nothing was lacking in the *math*, yet Azad was *Azad* (free) only. He found living here as if he was a prisoner. What a change from the life of a revolutionary young man to the dull life of a *math*! He found himself like a caged lion. Just in two months time he got fed up with this life. His patience too began to wear out. He had come under the impression that the *mahant* was sick and would soon pass away. Not to talk of his dying, he found the *mahant* improving and gaining strength by the day. Therefore, he wrote a letter to his friends: "I see no chances of the *mahant* dying. Your assessment was not correct. He is getting fat and healthy day by day. We should give up the hope that we would get the property of the *math*. Kindly permit me to be free from this bond."

The members of the party received the letter. They did not want to lose the property of the *math* at any cost. Therefore, immediately after the receipt of the letter, two more members, Govind Prakash and Manmath Nath Gupta reached Ghazipur in the guise of *Sadhus*. Govind Prakash became *guru* (head) and Manmath Nath Gupta *chela* (disciple). Both of them reached the *math*, met the *mahant*, and after that they met Azad. Then they went around in the *math* campus. The *math* was like a fort. The *math* was a completely suitable place for the programmes of the party, as it had high walls all around. It was a good property, and could be used to strengthen the party. Govind Prakash and Manmath Nath Gupta saw all this from various angles, and advised Azad to stay put there. Azad was resisting it, but both of his friends pressurised him very much, and made him practically helpless in the matter. Ultimately Azad had to bow to their wishes. Govind Prakash and Manmath Nath Gupta went back.

It is not easy to remain steadfast, if you are compelled to take a decision. Though Chandra Shekhar agreed to stay in the *math* under pressure form his friends at that time, but he could not bring his heart to that job. It became impossible for him to stay there. So one day without informing the *mahant*, Azad quietly freed himself from this bond, and reached Benares to his friends.

His friends were greatly disappointed at Azad's leaving the *math* in this manner. They felt that they have lost a treasure which was within their reach. The activities of the party could not be advanced due to paucity of funds. Now Azad again devoted himself to the organisation of the party. Though his hard work did bring in some money, but it was too meagre to do anything. So they thought of some new plans.

Collecting Subscription and Loan for the Party

'Hindustan Republican Association' entrusted Chandra Shekhar Azad chiefly the responsibility of collecting money. Azad got immersed in this work with all the zeal. He had a charming personality and was an adept in the art of conversation. So every one who came in his contact was impressed by him. Perhaps these qualities endeared him to Pandit Motilal Nehru. Books of history record that, though being at large for his role in various political episodes, Azad met him regularly and received financial assistance.

Pandit Motilal Nehru paid subscription to the party off and on. Rajarshi Purushottam Das Tandon always assisted the revolutionaries financially with a free hand. Nirmal Chand, the Attorney General, the famous litterateur Sharat Chandra of Calcutta, and Sir S.N. Sarkar, the Advocate General (Calcutta) and others regularly gave subscription to these revolutionaries. The number of members of the party was continuously increasing and consequently the expenses too shot up. Chandra Shekhar Azad and his friends had to face terrible deprivation in the absence of money. Sometime the situation was so bad that they had to go starving. They had to pass terribly cold weather in ordinary clothes. In spite of these deprivations the enthusiasm of these brave souls never slackened. They continued to advance unhindered the cause of the freedom of motherland. Azad had borrowed from his friends many times to further this cause. I am recounting here a few of these incidents which give an insight into their selfless love for the party. It is said that once the party needed money very urgently. Some pistols had to be bought. What to do? Azad was lost in finding a way out. A person came to them at noon and told them that Azad's parents were starving. He had collected some money from here and there, begging in the process. He gave that money to Azad for onward transmission to his parents.

Azad expressed his gratefulness to that man after receiving that money and, treating it as assistance from God, told the man—"I am thankful to you for this money. At this time the party needed this money most urgently. By God's grace, you have come at the most appropriate time."

That man was greatly surprised to hear the above words of Azad, and said, "Panditji, I have given you this money to help your parents. They are dying of hunger. But I don't understand why you want to spend it for your party?"

On this Azad said, "Pal (*Bhaiya*) Crores of people in the country are dying of hunger. I am not worried about my parents only, but for the whole country. Therefore, buying pistols at this time is absolutely necessary. In such a situation in the country if I care only for my family, that will be crass selfishness."

This reply of Azad made that man speechless, and he

went back.

Likewise on yet another occasion the party needed money very urgently. The president of the party placed this problem before Azad and told him that the party needed four thousand rupees immediately. If this money was not forthcoming the activity of the party would come to a stop. Realising the importance of the problem, Azad became serious, but he had not learnt to buckle down in the face of a difficulty. He took upon himself the responsibility of arranging the money and asked the president not to worry. He had a friend who dealt in money. He respected Azad greatly. Azad went to him. He posed his problem before his friend saying that he neeed four thousand rupees urgently, but his friend did not have money with him at that time. He said that he would arrange the money the next day. But Azad had given a word to his president to give the money on that day itself. Therefore, he told his friend that he required money immediately. He should arrange this money somehow, from somewhere, and Azad promised to return this money to him in six months with interest. His friend was in a dilemma. After that, his friend borrowed money from somebody and passed on rupees four thousand to Azad.

Like this, Azad arranged money for the needs of the party even if it involved borrowing. Chandra Shekhar and his friends lived a life of crippling poverty but the accounting of the party funds was kept with great care and honesty. Not a single paisa was misused.

Serving as a *Munim* (Accountant) in a Shop

Keeping the interests of the party in mind Chandra Shekhar Azad made a *mistry* (fitter) a member of the party. He was expert in making pistols. This solved a big problem of the party. Since the membership of the party had grown phenomenally, even borrowing and collecting subscription did not solve the financial worries. Many members of the party were in service and contributed a certain percentage/ share of their pay to the party funds. Taking a cue from this, Azad also started working as an accountant in a shop dealing with pickles and jams. Whatever he got from there as pay, he kept a very small share of it for himself, and the rest he gave to the party.

In this manner, Azad's entire life was dedicated to the party. He was continuously t ying to improve the finances of the party. Not only this, he took a leading role in all the activities of the party. That was why the party nicknamed him 'Quick Silver' i.e. mercury.

Poster of Revolution

Slowly and slowly the branches of 'Hindustan Republican Association' spread from Calcutta to Lahore in north India. Its centre was Benares. Ram Prasad Bismil performed the job of collecting weapons. All the weapons were collected in Benares and then sent to different branches. But carrying weapons such as guns and pistols from one place to another was not easy. They could be carried in first or second class compartments only. In spite of many difficulties, they were dispatched to various centres. Thus they collected a good stock of weapons at different centres. Now the party decided to warn the government.

A plan was made, and accordingly a poster was got printed. The poster mentioned the objectives of the party, along with an appeal to the public to revolt against the British government. According to the plan it was thoroughly discussed that the poster should be posted in all the cities on one fixed day. In the absence of this practice, the police could have been alerted and the posters seized, and the public would have remained ignorant of the objectives of the party. So, in January 1925 the public from Yangoon to Peshawar saw the poster on one fixed day. The members of the party themselves took the posters to all the cities. These posters were found pasted in every school, college, office, bazar, temple, mosque, church, gurudwara, cinema hall and other public places. The whole exercise was carried out with such care and secret that no one could know it.

The work of pasting the posters and their distribution in Benares was performed by Azad. He very cleverly manipulated the workers in the offices to his side and got the hand bills distributed by them. His work was appreciated in his party.

  Chandra Shekhar Azad : An Immortal Revolutionary of India

This activity made the Revolutionary Party famous in the whole country. No one had dreamt that the party was so extensive. This made the government really worried. Police and the Civil Intelligence Department of the government became determinedly busy in searching out the party.

3
Ends and Means

Even though the word 'revolution' is used today with other connotations such as 'The Green Revolution', 'The Industrial Revolution', it was initially meant to denote the change of power with violent means. To these travellers on the path of revolution the uppermost objective was to attain freedom for their country. They did not lay emphasis on the purity of means. Not only in India, the revolutionaries in Ireland and Soviet Union also had adopted violent means to attain their objective. These revolutionaries did not have any source of income, but they needed money to advance their cause. Despite getting subscriptions, the paucity of funds was always there. So under compulsion, they had to resort to dacoities also.

In the beginning of the 20th century the revolutionaries of Bengal had made dacoities a way of their operations. An article in *Yugantar*, an illustrious paper of Bengal, provides a peep into the reasoning that the revolutionaries did not consider dacoity improper in realising their sacred objectives.

One day in the morning a secret meeting of the representatives of various *mohallas* (localities, sectors etc.) of Calcutta was held at the residence of Subodh Malik. The incident relates to the year 1906-7. P. Mitra presided over this meeting. A resolution was mooted to commit dacoities to collect money for the secret committee. Some persons suggested that instead of committing dacoity at the residences of countrymen, it should be committed at the government treasuries. On this, others suggested that in order to have resources enabling one to loot the government treasuries, they would have to commit dacoities at the countrymen initially. It was clear that the rich would not part with their money for this. Later on Shri Aurobindo Ghosh reasoned that the political mistake that is being supposed in dacoity for independence was totally unfounded. In the end a representative from Rangpur suggested that a complete and accurate account of the looted booty be kept and that it would be returned to the persons concerned after India's independence. Aurobindo Ghosh endorsed this resolution and it was carried.

These revolutionaries observed this rule in all respects. A receipt of this money was despatched to the person whose money was looted. In 1916 a dacoity was committed in the Gopi Rai area of Calcutta. It was led by Shri Atulya Ghosh and Pulin Banerjee. Later on a letter sent to the owner of the house looted mentioned: "In our record of funds Rs. 9,891 and 5 pies are credited in your account. On India attaining independence this money will be refunded to you with interest.'

Focusing light on the propriety of these dacoities, Shri Manmath Nath Gupta expresses similar thoughts in his book *Bhagat Singh Aur Unka Yug* (Bhagat Singh and his Period). He wants to say that the revolutionaries stole ornaments from their own houses for the party. In Bengal a revolutionary caused a dacoity to be committed at his home. Money was accounted for scrupulously. Chandra Shekhar et al lived a life of utter poverty. Irish and Russian revolutionaries also committed dacoities. Stalin was involed in a dacoity near Baku, Krassin; the first ambassador of the Soviet Union to England was also involved in dacoities. The foreign revolutionaries termed it as forcibly collected subscription. According to a report of the Sedition Committee, the revolutionaries after committing a dacoity left a receipt behind stating that a particular amount had been taken. The loan would be paid off after India attained freedom.

Dacoities for the Activities of the Party

Left with no other option, the party resorted to dacoities. Pandit Ram Prasad Bismil led the party in dacoities. The first dacoity on behalf of the party was committed in the house of a *mukhia* (chief) of a village near Pratap Garh. Ram Prasad, along with his colleagues, left for commiting dacoity. They met some persons of that village, just outside the village. The villagers asked them where they were headed. In reply they told them that they were invited at the *mukhia's* house for a feast. Chandra Shekhar Azad was also a member of this group. On reaching the *mukhia's* house but before the dacoity, Bismil directed his colleagues: "The aim of the party is to get money, and not murdering anybody. Therefore, only money is to be looted. Please take care that no woman is maltreated in any way." Members entered the house and Ram Prasad Bismil stood outside with a pistol in his hand, so that if somebody from outside came to help, he could be stopped from getting in.

Members started looting-robbing inside. A hue and cry ensued from the house. Instructions were that no force would be applied while dealing with women. Taking advantage of this kind of conduct a woman seized the pistol from the hands of Chandra Shekhar Azad. The woman could not be struck or pounced upon. On hearing the hue and cry many villagers had gathered outside the home and their number was increasing. Ram Prasad Bismil stood blocking their entry. Situation became serious but no one was to be killed. Then Bismil motioned to his colleagues to clear out of there. Immediately all members made good their escape. They could not lay their hands on anything. On the contrary, they lost a pistol. So the party had to face a failure in the first dacoity itself.

The next dacoity was at the house of a *zamindar* (landlord). All the revolutionaries started looting inside the house. In the meanwhile a member of the gang espied a young girl there. Lust overpowered him and he started misbehaving with the girl. Chandra Shekhar saw this and warned that member to desist from it. But he did not pay heed to Azad's words. Upright Azad could not bear it. He grew red with anger and shot at that member of his group. Then he apologised to that girl for the unseemly conduct with her, and left that place without looting. So, they did not get anything in the second dacoity also.

Azad had taken a loan of four thousand rupees from his friend for party work. This money was to be returned to his friend with interest after six months. This has been mentioned in the last chapter. His friend had borrowed this money from somebody else to give to Azad. Only three months had pssed when that friend came to see Azad and told him that the person, from whom he had borrowed for Azad, was demanding his money back. So he requested Azad to return the money. This put Azad in a very embarrassing situation. He explained the situation to his friend, assuring that according to his promise the money would definitely be passed on to him after six months.

On this Azad's friend explained his helplessness to him and said that since he himself did not have any money on him, he could not return it to the lender. And returning was absolutely necessary. Realising the difficulty and helplessness of his friend, Azad gave him a word that the money would be sent to his home shortly.

The word given to the friend had to be honoured. But wherefrom was the money to be found? After being tossed in this dilemma for some time, Azad came to a conclusion. He charted out a plan in his mind.

Now Azad was in Delhi. He ventured out at noon to transform his plan into action and reached Chandni Chowk. It is one of the busiest and crowded places in Delhi. He had with him 5 or 6 party members also. Dressed in new and beautiful clothes, Azad reached in front of a jeweller's shop. He asked his colleagues to stand out, and himself went inside the shop. Once inside he engaged the jeweller in a discussion about various topics, and of course regarding the price of different ornaments. Then on a hint from him, his gang-members also entered the shop. People around him just did not know what happened, but Azad decamped from the jeweller's shop with a loot of fifteen thousand rupees.

Four thousand rupees were returned to his friend on time. After receiving the money when his friend wanted to know as to wherefrom the money was received, he told him the whole story. On this his friend remarked that it was not proper to loot money in this manner from innocent, unsuspecting people. It should be considered a sin. In response Azad said: "For me first comes the freedom of the country. I do not consider the looting of the rich a sin. They grow rich on sucking the blood of the poor public. In fact the wealth amassed by them belongs to the country. It is no sin to use this money for the good of the country." His friend became speechless on hearing this.

The entire revolutionary life of Chandra Shekhar Azad can be divided into two parts. Upto the Kakori episode he continued as a member of 'Hindustan Republican Association.' Here he worked under the leadership of Shachindra Nath Sanyal, with revolutionaries such as Ram Prasad Bismil as his comrades. This can be called as the first half of his revolutionary life. After this he carried out his revolutionary activities in association with Bhagat Singh et al. This will be called the second half of his life.

Duping as the Secretary to the Governor

There were plans of dacoities in the second half of his life, but Bhagat Singh was not in favour of dacoities on public. So dacoities were not committed, but ordinarily money was defintiely collected through other means. Now he himself was the president of his party. Once he had cornered fifteen thousand rupees from a *seth* (a moneyed man) in Kanpur, acting as the secretary to the Governor.

It happened like this: It was 9.00 P.M. Seth Dilsukh Rai was sitting with his *munim* and looking into his books of accounts. Then the servant of the *seth* told him that a gentleman wanted to see him. The *seth* asked his *munim* to go out and talk to him. The *munim* came out to talk, and later went in to tell the *seth* that the Governor's secretary had come to see him. He had a clerk and a peon also with him. "They want to see you right now." On hearing this the *seth* himself came out, received them respectfully and took them in. They were seated with great respect. With folded hands the *seth* enquired the reason of his visit. On this the secretary saheb said, "The government has run short of money due to war. So the government is collecting subscription from the high and wealthy persons. Therefore, I have come to you to ask for subscription on behalf of the Governor."

"Why did you undertake all this trouble? You could just call us. It would have been our pleasure to be present ourselves", said the *seth.*

"I came to you or you came to me are just one and the

same thing. What difference does it make?"

"This is your greatness, Sir, that you have been gracious to come to my place. Please tell me how much service I am supposed to do?"

"*Seth Ji*, Governor *saheb* himself has fixed the subscription amount after perusing your income-tax. So, fifteen thousand rupees are mentioned against your name."

The amount was somewhat heavy. Seeing the Seth a bit dejected the secretary saheb played another trick. "You are not an ordinary man. This amount is not on the higher side, in view of the income-tax you pay. His Excellency, the Governor is very highly pleased with you and proposes to honour you with the title of *Rai Bahadur* in the coming year."

The happiness of Seth Dilkhush Rai knew no bounds the moment the Seth heard of the title of the *Rai Bahadur*. Taking advantage of the situation, secretary *saheb* spoke again: "Your name figures in the list of the people on whom this title is going to be conferred next year. Just take it for granted that you have become the *Rai Bahadur*. Now only the formality has to be completed."

To be conferred with the title of tl.e *Rai Bahadur* was considered a matter of great honour in those days. On hearing the intended conferment of such a big honour in this manner, the seth was finding it difficult to contain his happiness. His heart was conjuring up visions of ecstasy and untold joy. He hardly knew what was racing in his mind. On this side the secretary saheb and his accomplices were also understanding what was going on in the mind of the Seth, and were laughing to themselves. They praised the Seth like anything, and convinced him that now nobody could snatch that title from him. Just in no time the Seth passed on the subscription of fifteer thousand rupees. Secretary saheb had brought the r(eipt book with him. The accompanying clerk prepared lie receipt and gave it to the Seth. Secretary saheb left im nediately with his clerk and the peon. The poor Seth was getting mad with happiness on the imminent title of the *Rai Bahadur*.

After a short while, the servant informed the Seth that the police had come. Just then a C.I.D. inspector entered along with four-five constables. As soon as he entered, he asked the Seth, "Who was here just a short while ago?"

"Governor saheb's secretary came. Asking for subscription", replied the Seth.

"Who else were with him?"

"He had a clerk and a peon with him."

The inspector asked about their height, face, features, complexion etc. The Seth gave a detailed description. Then the inspector asked, "Did you give them some subscription?"

"Yes, sir", said the Seth.

"How much?"

"Fifteen thousand rupees."

The inspected said, "You have been duped, Seth ji. A big fraud has been perpetrated on you. All the three were not the secretary, the clerk and the peon. They were Chandra Shekhar Azad, Bhagat Singh and Rajguru."

The Seth was cut to the quick. He saw the earth dizzying around him. He could hardly believe his ears. He was defrauded of fifteen thousand rupees just for nothing. He was angry with his *munim*. More than that, he was cursing himself for his foolishness.

Dacoity in Garodia Store

Azad continued with the activities of the party, after the arrest of Bhagat Singh. Many of the factories manufacturing bombs were still running, though the main members of the party had been arrested. Chandra Shekhar could not sit idle, particularly in trying times. A dacoity was committed at a motor company in Delhi on 6th June, 1930 to make up the shortage of funds. It is known as the Garodia Store Dacoity. Chandra Shekhar Azad himself led this operation. Other members of the party who accompanied him were Kashi Ram, Vidya Bhushan et al. They got thirteen thousand rupees in this dacoity.

The happy and surprising aspect of this dacoity was that when the owner of the store came to know that the dacoits were the revolutionaries, he did not pursue the matter further for investigation. This dacoity was exposed after the Lahore episode, in which one member of the party, Kailash Pati, turned approver.

Kakori Episode

The party was short of money in spite of every possible effort by its members. Consequently the activities of the party could not be carried out in time or efficiently. So the party decided to take a bold step. Pandit Ram Prasad Bismil has, in his autobiography, described this aspect as following:

"At this time the finances of the *samiti* were in a very bad shape. Arrangement of money was absolutely necessary. But how to do it? Charity was not forthcoming. Raising fund was an impossible dream. Seeing no way out, it was decided to commit a dacoity. We did not consider it desirable to loot the property of a particular person. So we thought, if looting was the only option, why should we not loot the government property or good? With these turbulence in mind one day I was travelling by train. I was in a compartment next to that of the guard. Station master came with a bag and dumped it in the guard's cabin. There was some noise as if an article was being moved; descending I saw a steel box. I thought to myself that the bag would be placed in it. On the next station I saw the guard putting the bag in the box. I guessed that the steel box in the cabin should be tied in chains, locked and when required it could be taken out after unlocking the chain. After a few days I was at Lucknow railway station. I saw that the coolies were taking out the box containing cash from a train. A close look revealed that they were not chain-locked in the cabin. They were just placed there. I decided there and then that it would be my smart kill. I was seized of this idea. Immediately I moved on to where the time-table was displayed on the platform and guessed that the train, originating from Saharanpur, must collect daily ten thousand rupees till it reached Lucknow."

It is clear that this plan was Pandit Ram Prasad Bismil's brainchild. So, 9th August, 1925 was fixed for executing it. Ten members of the party were selected for it—Pandit Ram Prasad Bismil, Ashfaqullah Khan, Rajendra Nath Lahiri, Chandra Shekhar Azad, Manmath Nath Gupta, Banwari Lal, Shachindra Nath Bakshi, Murari Lal, Keshav Chakravarti, and Mukundi Lal.

8 Down Passenger train started from Saharanpur, and it carried revenue collected from all wayside stations to

Lucknow. So, these brave persons left for their expedition at a fixed hour. In this respect, Manmath Nath Gupta writes, "On the evening of 9th, we boarded the train at Shahjahanpur armed with chisel, hammers etc. This train carried under the escort of armed guards some other government treasury funds also in addition to railway funds. There were other armed men also in the train. Many white platoons with arms were also present, along with a Major in 1st class. When our scouts passed all this information to us, we were in a fix. Shri Ashfaq possibly tried to bring his earlier objections to weigh them carefully but we were determined. We had advanced so much in our scheme that our return was very difficult, and we did not want to return either. An important thing was that though Ashfaq was advancing his objections, but when he realised that he was not having his way and found us determined to execute the plan, he braced himself to do it wholeheartedly. His big, beautiful eyes lit up and he presented himself to play his role with unusual courage and enthusiasm."

Shri Ashfaqullah, Rajendra Lahiri and Shachindra Nath Bakshi travelled in IInd class, while others occupied IIIrd class. Some members were put in IInd class with a specific purpose. The train had to be stopped at Kakori by pulling chain, because chains in IIIrd class compartments were generally out of order.

This group had four new Mouser pistols, more than fifty rounds of cartridges for each of them and some other miscellaneous weapons. Kakori is a small village in Lucknow district. A small distance away from it, the train was stopped by pulling the chain. When the train stopped, passengers disembarked and moved towards the guard's cabin. Some started peeping out of windows, looking for the reason of stoppage. Then the guard also came down, and started moving towards the compartment from which the chain was pulled. The revolutionaries came down from their compartments immediately. They ordered the passengers to get into the compartments, but asked the guard to lie down on the ground so that the train could not proceed without him. At some distance on both sides of the track, two persons (on each side) stood with Mouser pistols in hand, which could fire upto a thousand yards. They were asked to fire in the air intermittently, but one young man fired in front which killed a passenger. That person was perhaps going towards a ladies compartment, trying to reassure his wife.

The rest of the members of the group climbed into the guard's cabin. The steel box was taken out. It was broken open. The bags coming out of it were put into a bundle made of sheet. Just at this time some mail or express train was coming from Lucknow side. The revolutionaries started entertaining a doubt that it might stop and may be it carried some armed persons also. Shri Manmath Nath Gupta describes this incident thus:

"Bags were taken out and bundled in a sheet. At this time some mail or express train was coming from Lucknow side. That train was passing at a very fast speed. Our hearts were pounding. We thought if this train stopped and a few armed men descended, then a few of us are sure to be killed. Thank God, the train somehow passed. We hid our guns when the train was passing by our side, but when the train had passed, we were back on our job. We completed the whole operation in a very shorttime, possibly ten minutes, and moved towards the bushes with bags."

After this loot, the revolutionaries moved towards Lucknow. On their way, they took the money out and threw the empty leather bags in a pond formed out of rain water and proceeded towards Lucknow. This group of the youth did not face any opposition in this dacoity, even though there were fourteen armed men in the train. There were two white armed men as well. The driver and the engineer of the train hid themselves in toilet out of fear. The passengers were told not to worry as nobody would disturb them, only the government treasury would be looted. So they kept quiet. The passengers in the train thought that the train had been surrounded by a large posse, whereas this was done by ten youth only, of an age group of mostly 20-22 years. Of course, all these young men were healthy and strong.

The party was liberated from the burden of debts on one hand due to the success of this dacoity while on the other the courage and confidence of the youth soared. New weapons were bought and future plans were drawn up.

Series of Arrests

The Kakori episode was like an open challenge to the government. Soon the police became active. Raids and searches were carried out at different places. C.I.D. also got busy in the search at its own level. Soon forty persons were arrested, whereas only ten persons had participated in the dacoity. Persons completely unrelated to this case were also arrested. They were, however, later let off.

Banwari Lal and Indra Bhushan Mitra of Shahjahanpur and Gopi Mohan of Kanpur were also arrested. Of these the first two became approvers, and Gopi Mohan Saha agreed to become the government witness. Banwari Lal, a participant of this dacoity, became a confessing witness. He told the police everything. The police did not get any approver of the Benares Centre. Therefore, the police could not get any information about this centre.

Barring the above referred four persons, the rest twenty-four persons were successfully proved as convicts. Twenty one were arrested, and Ashfaqullah Khan, Chandra Shekhar Azad and Shachindra Nath Bakshi, who could not be arrested by the police, were declared absconders.

Later on Damodar Swarup was released on grounds of serious illness. The case was withdrawn for some unknown, mysterious reasons against Shiv Charan Lal of Mathura-Agra Centre and Veerbhadra Tiwari of Orai-Kanpur Centre.

Case

A case was instituted against the rest of the accused on the following charges:

1. Under Section 121:   Declaration of war against the British Emperor.
2. Under Section 120:   Non-political conspiracy.
3. Under Section 396:   Murder and Dacoity.
4. Under Section 302:   Murder.

Pandit Jagat Narayan Mulla pleaded the case on behalf of the government. He was paid five hundred rupees per day. Pandit Govind Ballabh Pant, Shri Bahadurji, Chandra Bhanu Gupta and Mohan Lal Saxena and others defended the accused. The government spent something upwards of rupees ten lakhs of this case.

Shri Ashfaqullah Khan and Shri Shachindra Nath Bakshi were arrested later. Therefore, a separate case was filed against them.

Sentences

The accused of the Kakori episode received the following sentences in both the cases:

Death Sentence: Pandit Ram Prasad Bismil, Thakur Roshan Singh, Rajendra Nath Lahiri and Ashfaqullah Khan.

Deportation (*Kala Pani*): Shachindra Nath Sanyal and Shachindra Nath Bakshi.

14 Years' Imprisonment: Manmath Nath Gupta.

10 Years' Imprisonment: Yogesh Chandra Chatterjee, Mukundi Lal, Govind Charan Kar, Raj Kumar Singh, and Ram Krishna Khatri.

Seven Years' imprisonment: Vishnu Sharan Dublish, and Suresh Bhattacharya.

Five Years' imprisonment: Bhupendra Nath Sanyal, Prem Krishna Khanna and Ram Dularey Dwivedi.

Four Years' Imprisonment: Pranavesh Chatterjee.

Though Banwari La had become a confessing witness, he could not escape punishment. The court sentenced him to five years of imprisonment.

The government went into appeal against Manmath Nath Gupta, Yogesh Chandra Chatterjee, Mukundi Lal, Govind Charan Kar, Vishnu Sharan Dublish and Suresh Bhattacharya. Out of these six accused, Yogesh Chandra Chatterjee, Mukundi Lal and Govind Charan Kar who were earlier awarded ten years' imprisonment, were deported, and whereas Vishnu Sharan Dublish and Suresh Bhattacharya, who were earlier awarded seven years' imprisonment, got enhanced imprisonment of ten years. Manmath Nath Gupta's sentence remained as it was, due to his being under-age.

After the Judgement

The whole country raised its voice against this judgement.

Agitations and demonstrations were staged throughout the country for cancelling the death sentence. The members of the Central Assembly, through a signature campaign, appealed the Viceroy for mercy. Twice the dates for hanging were got postponed. An appeal was filed in the Privy Council also, but the result was zero. At long last the British government demonstrated its cruelty. Rajendra Lahiri was hanged in Gonda jail on 17th December, 1927. On 19th December Ram Prasad Bismil was hanged in Gorakhpur jail and Ashfaqullah Khan in Faizabad jail, and Thakur Roshan Singh was hanged on 18th December in Allahabad jail.

In this way this party was shattered. Chandra Shekhar Azad alone evaded the police which could not trace or arrest him. With this the first half of Azad's revolutionary life came to an end.

4
The Intervening Period

After the Kakori episode Chandra Shekhar Azad alone was the person whom the police could not arrest in spite of its innumerable efforts. Right up to the day of judgement in the Kakori episode even the members of the party did not know where Azad was. According to Manmath Nath Gupta, after this episode, Azad told the members of the party that he was leaving for home, but nobody, including the members of his party, knew whether his home was in Unnao or Bhabhra.

In this episode all the friends of Azad were arrested. The police searched everywhere, including the most unlikely places such as wells, ponds etc. Regarding this Dr. Bhagwan Das Mahore writes:

"The most powerful and resourceful British government left no stone unturned in its efforts to arrest him. Award of many thousand rupees was declared for his head. It is said all the wells were searched, all the rivers were dived into, and the caves were visited. But Azad lived in utmost tranquillity with Rudra Narayan."

Jhansi and the adjoining area was the place of his residence during this period. The centre of the party at Jhansi was the place of his hiding these days. In a situation like this it was required that one kept quiet for some time. The period after the Kakori episode and before the formation of a new party by Bhagat Singh is called the intervening period of Azad's revolutionary life. Following were his activities during this period:

In Jhansi

While at large, first he reached Jhansi. Here he learnt the work of motor driving and mechanic, and worked in

Bundelkhand Motor Company. While working here, he met with a small mishap. There was a car which did not start. It was so stiff or jammed that no one could rotate its handle. In order to start it, Azad rotated its handle with such a force that his hand was dislocated. He was immediately taken to a hospital. Azad had to be rendered unconscious by anaesthesia for operation. But this advice of the doctors left Azad worried, because he had heard that under an unconscious state sometimes a man blurts out his secrets. Therefore, Azad agreed to undergo the operation while remaining conscious. But doctors did not accept this. Azad got down the operation table. Then his friends somehow persuaded him to consent to the use of anaesthesia.

It seems that during his unconsciousness he slipped something out for the doctor to know that he was a revolutionary. The doctor talked to him with great respect after the operation. While discharging him from the hospital the doctor said, "Now your hand is all right. Don't worry. I hope you will use your hands bravely for your country."

Azad lived with Master Rudra Narayan in Jhansi, posing as his younger brother. According to Dr. Mahore, the police raided the house of Rudra Narayan many times, but they could not arrest Azad even though he stood before them. The reason was that the conduct of Azad was such as the police could not imagine that he was Azad. The police did not have any photograph of Azad with them to recognise him.

"Rudra Narayan's home was searched again and again. But Azad, who lived completely openly, could not be arrested. Azad joked with the officers and the policemen who had come raiding. He regaled them with the stories, detailing the tricks of rogue Azad. When the policemen went away, Azad would tell us, laughing—"These buggers have made me a demon and magician. These are very ordinary men. They stand like slaves before a magistrate: Now, think of that Kumudi Singh who was saying that the revolutionaries came from high families. From this point of view, well, Ashfaqullah can be considered a Deputy Magistrate."

In Jhansi, along with working for the motor company, Azad would go to jungle and practise shooting. He was in regular touch with Bhagwan Das Mahore during this period.

In the Guise of a Sadhu (Mendicant)

After this Azad started living in a hut outside Dhimarpur village, in the guise of a *sadhu* (mendicant). Rudra Narayan had advised him to this effect. Here he recited the quartets (*chaupai*) from *Ram-Charit Manas*. In the beginning people used to bring food for him to his hut, but later on Azad went to the homes of the devouts to take his food. Here he started a school also to educate small children. In the beginning the school functioned under the open sky, but later on a rich *thakur* of the village, Malkhan Singh, gave him the drawing room of his house for this purpose. Afterwards Azad, who was known as *Brahmachari*, began to live in the house of Malkhan Singh. The reason was that Malkhan Singh and his three brothers were in service, and lived away from home. The house was also safe if a male member lived there. Azad, in fact, became one of their family members.

In Contact with Rulers/Kings

In this period Azad came in contact with many kings and *zamindars*. Once the king of Orchha was in the jungle, hunting along with his *divan* (minister). He met Azad, who was dressed as a *sadhu*. Realising that the Raja Saheb was going for hunting, Azad expressed his desire to accompany him. The *Raja* was greatly surprised to see a *sadhu* expressing his desire for hunting. On this Azad said that he was only a *pujari*. A gun was given to him. The *Raja Saheb* and his attendants laughed at this. While hunting everyone occupied his post. There was a strong, wild boar. The *Raja* and his attendants shot at it, but everyone missed his aim. Then in the end Azad aimed, and killed it in the first shot itself. This incident fully convinced *Raja Saheb* that he was not a *sadhu* or *pujari* but a revolutionary. *Raja Saheb* himself had sympathies with the freedom fighters. This introduction turned into a friendship. Azad communicated the reality about himself after many days to the *Raja Saheb*.

Once a *Lat Saheb* (lord) was coming to Orchha. Azad got a message conveyed to the *Raja* that he wanted to welcome him in his own style. The *Raja Saheb* politely asked Azad that since the *Lat Saheb* was coming as a guest of his state, he (Azad) should not do anything just out of the way.

It is also reported that this *Raja Saheb*, under the influence of one of his servants who was very close to him, had agreed to get Azad arrested. When the *Raja* and his servant were discussing this plan, Azad was sleeping in his palace. He was snoring heavily so that the *Raja* did not suspect. Afterwards as soon as he got a chance, he made good his escape from there.

Master Rudra Narayan had advised Azad to live like a *sadhu*. With his co-operation he came in contact with the *Raja Saheb* Khaniadhana also. Azad had first gone to him as an expert motor mechanic. He told *Raja Saheb* later on that he was a revolutionary. In March, 1928 the *Raja Saheb* had given him this assurance also that he would give him some weapons for the activities of the party.

Bhagwan Das Mahore also lived with him during this period. Azad had become a strong confidante of *Raja Saheb* Kalkaji Singhdev. Here he practised driving and hunting also. *Raja Saheb* used to go for hunting also with him. The relatives and workers of *Raja Saheb* became jealous of this intimacy of Azad with the *Raja Saheb*. Azad left Khaniadhana as a consequence.

In Bombay

Some books describe that after Bundelkhand Azad again went to Bombay and he worked there as a coolie at the port. During the day he was busy loading and unloading cargo in the ships, for which he got nine annas in the evening as wages. He would see a movie till twelve in the night, and then slept either in a godown or on a footpath. This continued for about a year and a half.

Here he met Veer Savarkar. Savarkar acquainted him with the difficulties in the path of revolution and advised him not to be afraid of them. Azad got a new inspiration from it, and he headed north from Bombay to re-organise a new party *de novo*.

5

A Fresh Start: Re-organisation of the Party

The Kakori episode proved to be a curse upon 'Hindustan Republican Association'. All the main members of the party were arrested. Out of them four were awarded the death sentence, and the rest were sentenced to long imprisonments. Only Azad was left, or could save himself. He faced the problem of re-organising the party, and he plunged himself into it heart and soul. Luckily he got good friends like Bhagat Singh for this work. The second half of his revolutionary life starts here.

Meeting with Bhagat Singh

Azad reached Kanpur in connexion with the re-organisation of the party. Here he stayed with the illustrious freedom fighter, journalist and social reformer Ganesh Shankar Vidyarthi. Bhagat Singh had also come there. Here they met for the first time. Shri Yash Pal, describing this meeting, wrote in *Singhavalokan*:

"As soon as Azad entered the inner room, he saw an unknown but brilliant young man sitting next to Shri Vidyarthi. Azad hesitated for a moment on seeing him. That young man had a lean and thin body and tall stature. He had a fair colour and small eyes. He gave an impression of uniqueness from his face. He had put on a turban, tossed and hanging on his loose hair. He had a coat and a lungi on his body. He attracted Azad."

"Please come in, Pandit ji", pat came Shri Vidyarthi's hospitality, seeing Azad hesitant.

The busy young man raised his eyes and looked up. He saw an imposing young man of grand personality in the form of Panditji.

After that both were introduced to each other. Both shared common thoughts. Both were impressed by each other. This first meeting of theirs converted into a life-long friendship. It was a historic meeting. It was an unbreakable union of two persons crazy for their motherland, and who worked together in future shoulder to shoulder for the attainment of India's freedom, and who created a new history. In fact, the second half of the revolutionary life of *Veer* Chandra Shekhar Azad started after he met Bhagat Singh.

A New Party: Hindustan Samajwadi Ganatantrik Sena

Chandra Shekhar Azad, Bhagat Singh and their other friends got busy in the organisation of a new revolutionary party. For this, contact was established with revolutionary parties in all the states of North India. Shiv Verma went to Bengal and met the revolutionaries there in this context. They requested the revolutionaries to co-operate with their party, but the Bengali revolutionaries chose to propose some terms and conditions for this co-operation. The first condition was that the members of all the states joining this new party will have to work under the command of the leader of the Bengal party, and they would be under obligation to accept every thing their Bengali leaders said. The second condition was that the new party would initially, concentrate on recruiting members only, collect money and weapons, and would do nothing that attracted the government's attention to it. The youths, desirous of forming the new party, did not accept these conditions. They were opposed to this kind of dictatorship. Though, as an aim, they wanted to unite the parties in all the states, they wanted to organise the new party in a democratic manner. This party of Bengal wanted its 'monopoly', but it hardly had any influence on the public or discipline of their own. When Shiv Verma went to Bengal to establish contact with them, the Bengalis could even not arrange for their stay. So any co-operation with them was given up.

On 6th December, 1928 the revolutionaries organised a

meeting in the ruins of Feroz Shah Kotla Fort for the formation of a new party. (Different dates are mentioned in different books, but most of them mention the above date.) This was attended by the representatives of all the states of North India except Bengal. Bhagat Singh and Sukhdev were the representatives of Punjab. Kundan La represented Rajasthan, Shiv Verma, Brahma Dutt Misra, Jai Dev, Vijay Kumar Sinha and Surendra Pande represented United Provinces (Uttar Pradesh), and Phamindra Nath Ghosh and Manmohan Banerjee were the representatives of Bihar. For some unknown and unavoidable reasons Chandra Shekhar Azad could not attend this meeting, but he had already conveyed to Bhagat Singh and Shiv Verma that he would accept any decision taken by majority opinion in this meeting.

Till then the revolutionary parties of different states had their separate names. So after uniting all the parties of different states, a new all India party was formed. The name given to this new organisation was '*Hindustan Samajwadi Ganatantrik Sena*'. All the members of this party were new. Though in a way Chandra Shekhar Azad was just a young man, yet earlier he had the privilege of working with Ram Prasad Bismil in 'Hindustan Republican Association' and had gained substantial experience of using weapons whereas the other members were completely unexperienced in this regard. Therefore he was made the Supreme Commander of '*Hindustan Samajwadi Ganatantrik Sena*'—its Commander-in-Chief.

Central Committee of the New Party

A Central Committee of the new party was constituted, with representatives from each state. It had the following members:

1.	Bhagat Singh	(Punjab)
2.	Chandra Shekhar	(United Provinces)
3.	Sukhdev	(Punjab)
4.	Shiv Verma	(United Provinces)
5.	Vijay Kumar	(United Provinces)
6.	Phanindra Nath Ghosh	(Bihar)
7.	Kundan Lal	(Rajasthan)

It was clear in the formation of this party that no single individual would have control over it. All the property of the party would be under the Central Committee. The Central Committee would deliberate and decide before any course of action was taken. All decisions would be taken on the basis of majority. The word '*samajwadi*' was added to the name of the party with a specific purpose. It indicated that this party would strive for the establishment of a society based on the socialistic principles of Marxism, and would remove exploitation.

These issues were also discussed in this meeting that the party would wage an armed struggle for the freedom of India, which would require money in a compulsory form. Since it was a secret movement, it was not possible to collect money through subscription. It was decided that dacoities would be resorted to, to solve this problem. Besides, it was also decided that as far as possible dacoities should be committed at the government banks, treasuries and post offices. Committing dacoities in individual homes deprived the party the sympathy of the public. Therefore, this was considered harmful for the party.

Provincial and Inter-Provincial Organisation of the Party

Discussion was carried out regarding provincial and inter-provincial organisation also of the party. Bhagat Singh and Vijay Kumar were assigned inter provincial responsibility, so that the relations between units of various states were on an even keel and good. In addition to this, the organising representatives of all provinces were also appointed. Shiv Verma for United Provinces, Sukhdev for Punjab, Phanindra Nath for Bihar and Kundan La for Rajputana were appointed as organising representatives.

Thus Chandra Shekhar got the honour of being the president of the new organisation 'Hindustan Samajwadi Ganatantrik Sena'. Seen from one angle, there was no difference in the objectives of this organisation and the earlier organisation 'Hindustan Republican Association.' But the name of the earlier party did not denote its objectives. In this context, Manmath Nath Gupta writes:

"In the Kakori period the name of the committee was

'Hindustan Republican Association'. It was felt that the name conveyed less sense, i.e. it was thought that the name did not fully express the objectives of the party. Therefore, it had to be more expressive, and accordingly the name given to the new party was 'Hindustan Republican Socialist Army' i.e. Hindustan Samajwadi Prajatantrik Sena. In brief, it resulted from the fact that the growth in the revolutionary movement was registered more in objectives than in means. Accordingly, the name changed. This change indicates more growth in the objectives of the party. The party declared socialism and the leadership of the proletariat as its objectives."

Hide and Seek with the Police

After being at large due to the Kakori episode, Azad had not even seen his mother for about two years. His father had died. The old mother had come to live in Kanpur. Her heart was crying to see her only son. She knew that Azad had gone underground after some dacoity. Many of his friends had either been hanged in punishment or were undergoing long terms of imprisonment. If caught, Azad too was bound to be sentenced. One day Azad came to see his mother. The mother and son had met after such a long time. Just a short while later, Bhagat Singh and Sukhdev also reached there. Bhagat Singh told him that the police had found him out. Therefore, they should run away immediately. But Azad was used to playing with dangers. He always carried a loaded pistol with him. He prepared himself to face the police. On this Bhagat Singh advised him that such audacity would land him in difficulty. Therefore, all were up and about and ran away.

Likewise, once he was sitting n Kanpur with Shri Ganesh Shankar Vidyarthi, the editor c *Pratap*. Then he learnt that the police had come to know of . is presence there. So, Azad and one of his friends left that p ace and went to the place of his mother's residence. After taking food both of his friends went to sleep. In the meanwhile, no sooner had Azad left Shri Vidyarthi than a police officer with a posse of constables reached there. Azad had already left that place. Somebody had informed the police that Azad had gone to his mother.

The police reached there also. The door was closed from inside. Seeing the police outside both the friends got up. Azad prepared himself to face the police.

Both the friends took out their pistols. The police was continuously knocking at the door. When the police officer saw that the door was not being opened, he ordered to break it open. They started breaking the door. As soon as one part of the door was broken, Azad and his friends started firing at the police. In reply the police also returned the fire, but both the friends saved themselves behind cover. Many policemen were wounded. The police officer got angry. He ordered the constables to get in. The door had completely broken. Scores of policemen, with their guns pointed, got ready to barge inside. On this side Azad and his friends had fired all the cartridges and now their pistols were empty. Before the police could enter, both of his friends climbed on the roof, and from there jumped on to the adjoining roof. The police surrounded that house also. It continued with firing as well. Both the revolutionaries retaliated with throwing bricks on them. Then his lone friend Shukla kept throwing bricks. Azad had already disappeared, jumping from one roof to another. The police was hoodwinked. It had thought that both the persons were throwing bricks. The police continued to fire at Shukla under this misconception. None paid any attention to Azad's running away. The police party climbed up to the roof. There was nothing except the dead body of Shukla. The police was searching everywhere; however, Azad reached the railway station in a changed dress and reached Delhi from there.

Sparing the Life of a Police Officer

A police officer, Tasadduq Hussein, was specifically assigned the task of arresting Azad. He was busy with all zeal to collect evidence against him. This fact was not unknown to Azad. Once he thought that he should be finished, but then he thought that it would be of no use. Once he is killed, some other person will take up that job.

This officer always followed him. When Azad reached Delhi, he also came there. He was with him like his shadow. So it was required that he be taught a lesson. One day, sensing an opportunity Azad himself came to him and confronted him with pistol placed on his chest. Tasadduq Hussein was awestruck. He sweated profusely. He was shaking from head to toe, seeing death in front of him in the form of Azad. In a voice choked with mortal fear he begged Azad to spare his life in the name of Allah, and vowed not to shadow him in future. On this Azad spared his life with a warning. After this, he never followed Azad.

Azad took great delight in doing such daring deeds. Once he was coming to Kanpur in disguise. The police knew this, and it was fully prepared. The railway station had been surrounded on all sides. A net of secret agents had been spread on platforms. The train coming from Lucknow stopped at the platform at its fixed time. Azad in disguise stepped out of his compartment and fearlessly walking though the secret agents reached the exit gate. An inspector was standing there. Before he could do anything, he put his hands in his pocket and stood aside for Azad to pass through. A smiling Azad came out of the gate and the police continued to look for him.

Plan for the Release of the Participants of the Kakori Kand

'Hindustan Socialist Republican Army' charted out a plan to get the brave participants of the Kakori Kand (event) released. Chandra Shekhar Azad, Vijay Kumar Sinha, Bhagat Singh, Raj Guru, Batukeshwar Dutt, Shiv Verma and Jai Dev reached Agra to execute the plan but could not succeed. Dr. Bhagwan Das Mahore was also a member of the group working for the release. He was a student then. Dr. Mahore writes about the failure of this plan:

"We were asked to come to Agra to get Shri Yogesh Chandra Chatterjee from jail. Plan was, when he comes out, he would be boldly snatched away. But could not succeed. Chatterjee was to be sent from one jail to another. But he was not sent."

After this also, some members of the group stayed behind in Agra, but the plan did not work. As a result, they too returned disappointed.

Likewise a plan was made to get Ram Prasad Bismil released. But he was under heavy police guard. So this plan too resulted in failure. The members of the party wanted to know more about him. Bhagat Singh wanted to get him released at all costs. In this context Shiv Verma writes—

'Two or three days later Vijay came and reported about the alertness and heavy police guard around Bismil, with the suggestion that we would have to give up the idea for the moment. This news dashed all hopes of Bhagat Singh. After a lot of search, they laid their hands on one *ghazal* (an Urdu poem with unrhymed lines).

Bismil was the leader of the *Kakori Kand*. Therefore, he was under the strictest police guard after the declaration of his sentence to death. There was a strict watch on what he received and what he sent out. The following *ghazal*, written by him, was perhaps considered an ordinary *ghazal* by the jail authorities. They could not get at the subtle inherent meaning. The *ghazal* goes like this:

"No use receiving salutations

After the death of one prone to dying.

No use receiving her message

When the heart is completely ruined.

When one has lost all hopes

When one has lost all thoughts

No use if the illustrious

Came with a message.

O my naïve heart!

Destroy thyself in the lane of the beloved

What's the use of prize

Received after my failures?

Wish, I could see in my life

my cherished dream.

What's the use if all

Denizens came walking to my tomb!

On the last night were the throes

of Bismil's heart worth seeing

It matters how, just for a name sake,

He had a breath or two in the morning.

It is clear from this *ghazal* that Bismil conveyed a message to his companions through these lines that they should make quick efforts to get freed the brave participants of this *kand* from being hanged. Otherwise it would be too late and they would be disappointed. These efforts were made in 1927.

6
The Rise and Fall: New Activities

The main objective of 'Hindustan Samajwadi Ganatantrik Sena' was to liberate India through an armed revolution. Azad was not particularly satisfied with all the activities so far. He wanted to make a powerful blast which would stir the whole country and terrify the British government. Coincidence created such a situation as the attention of the whole country was drawn towards the activities of the party. The Lahore Conspiracy, Assembly Bomb Explosion and throwing a bomb at Viceroy's train—all these were the activities of this party.

Arrival of the Simon Commission

On 8th November, 1927 the Viceroy announced that the Simon Commission was arriving in India from England to examine and evaluate the administrative reforms. No Indian was a member of this commission. Its president was Sir John Simon, a famous lawyer of England. This Commission reached India on 3rd February, 1928. These days the country was under a severe grip of communalism. All the political parties of India decided to boycott this commission. The whole country observed a total strike on the day of its arrival. Simon was opposed with black flags and the slogan 'Simon, Go Back', as soon as it landed in Bombay. When the commission arrived in Delhi, it was welcomed here also in the same way. The same was the situation in Madras. In fact, the police had to resort to firing there, which resulted in the death of three demonstrators. It was opposed in Calcutta also.

'Hindustan Samajwadi Ganatantrik Sena' had decided

to show its disappointment by throwing a bomb at the Simon Commission in Lahore, but this could not be executed due to paucity of funds with the organisation.

On 20th October, 1928 this Commission reached Lahore. Here Lala Lajpat Rai led the protesting demonstrators. Youth members of 'Naujawan Bharat Sabha' were in the forefront of the demonstrators. Bhagat Singh had founded 'Naujawan Bharat Sabha'. By this time this sabha had become a part of 'Hindustan Samajwadi Gantantrik Sena'. Its members were directed to work under the leadership of Lala Lajpat Rai in this boycott.

A vast crowd of protesters had gathered at the railway station waiting for the arrival of the commission. The Superintendent of Police of Lahore, Mr. Scott was present there with his full force and other officers. He deemed it proper to remove the crowd from there so that the commission could be escorted comfortably. He had assigned his Deputy Superintendent, Mr. Saunders, with this task, with the instruction to lathicharge people, if required, to clear the road. Saunders began with lathicharging. Demonstrators dispersed here and there. The road was cleared. But Lala Lajpat Rai stuck to his place along with members of 'Naujawan Bharat Sabha'. Saunders reported this to Scott, and ordered his constables to remove the crowd. The crowd did not budge from there. Then Saunders just swooped upon the crowd with lathicharge. There was an endless crowd behind Lalaji. Lathicharge was going on in front. Young men had surrounded Lalaji in defence. Then a charge of lathi from Saunders hit the umbrella of Lalaji. It broke. After this, Scott himself swooped upon the demonstrators like a hungry wolf. Lalaji received the blows of lathi on his head and shoulders. He was drenched in blood. On this Lalaji said, "Let the demonstration be suspended in opposition to the atrocious activities of the police." So, the demonstration was stopped on his orders.

The same evening meeting at the Morigate grounds, Lahore, was held in protest against the barbarous activity of the police. Then Lalaji in his address said:

"A government which carries on murderous attacks on unarmed public cannot be called a civilised government, and such government cannot stay. I challenge that the blow which the police of this government has given me today will finish off this government one day. I declare that the wounds I have received today will prove to be the last nail in the coffin of the British Rule in India."

Lalaji was taken to hospital after this, and there on 29th day, on 17th November, 1928 he died due to these injuries.

The whole country plunged into an ocean of sorrow on the death of Lalaji. The barbaric act of the police was condemned all around. The revolutionaries grew impatient to avenge this.

The Murder of Saunders

Some members of 'Hindustan Samajwadi Ganatantrik Sena' were present in Lahore at the time of death of Lalaji. They, therefore, began to plan to avenge this murder. All the activities of this party were carried out as per the majority decision of the members of its central committee. Though Phanindra Nath and Shiv Verma were not in Lahore, yet all other members favoured this plan. Decision had to be taken immediately, and since it was not possible to call these two members quickly, therefore in the first week of December, 1928 a meeting of the committee was held in a house in Majang Mohalla of Lahore and it was decided to avenge Lalaji's death.

Outlines of the Plan

A plan to kill the Police Superintendent, Scott, was drawn up. A group of five young men, Chandra Shekhar Azad, Bhagat Singh, Shiv Ram, Raj Guru and Jai Gopal, was charged with its execution. Jai Gopal was asked to keep a watch on the activities of Scott, his movement, routes etc. Jai Gopal kept a close vigil and kept scenting other related things.

On the fixed day, 15th December 1928, Jai Gopal was sent to the police station some time in advance. He reached there on a bicycle. He placed his bicycle on the gate in such a way as if something was wrong with it. Murder was to be done by Bhagat Singh and Raj Guru. Chandra Shekhar was hiding behind the wall of D.A.V. College, opposite to the gate of police station. The task entrusted to him was to stop the policemen who would chase Bhagat Singh and Raj Guru when they ran after killing Scott. He was an expert in it. The bicycle was to be used as a standby, in the likely event of the shot missing Scott. It could be used to follow him.

All the persons reached their fixed points at the scheduled time. Here a miscalculation crept in. Jai Gopal confused in identities and he mistook Saunders as Scott. As soon as Saunders reached the gate on his motor-cycle, Jai Gopal pointed and Raj Guru immediately shot him in the neck. Saunders at once fell down, along with his motorcycle. To ensure that he did not survive, Bhagat Singh hit his head with four or five shots. After completing the job both of them moved towards the D.A.V. College compound. On this, one constable, standing in the verandah of the police station, began shouting. Then traffic inspector Fern and two other constables ran and chased them. Bhagat Singh fired at Fern. He saved himself by ducking, but in the process he fell down. Other constables were startled but they continued chasing. On this Azad took out his Mouser pistol and warned them to run away. Chanan Singh, one of the two constables, wanted to show a little bit more bravery. So, he continued chasing. Then Azad fired. His shot hit Chanan Singh and he fell down for ever.

After the fall of Chanan Singh, none dared to give them a chase. Chandra Shekhar Azad, Bhagat Singh and Raj Guru reached the hostel of D.A.V. College. From there, Chandra Shekhar and Raj Guru exited from the back gate riding a bicycle. Bhagat Singh donned the coat, pant and hat of a friend, took some money also from him and left.

Now the police had become fully alert. Lahore was surrounded on all sides, and sealed. It is worth noting that when Bhagat Singh fired at Fern who was following him, then two constables had seen and recognised him. So it was difficult for him to leave the city. Keeping this in mind he got himself a hair cut and got his beard shaved.

Escape from Lahore

Soon one by one, all the members of the party who had

gathered in Lahore left for Ferozpur, Amritsar etc., but it was not easy for these three to leave. So a special strategy was devised for this purpose. It has already been told that Bhagat Singh became a *mona* (a Sikh without a beard), so a drama had to be played to get out of Lahore. Help was taken from Smt. Durga Devi, the wife of famous revolutionary Bhagwati Charan Verma. She herself was a revolutionary and a member of this party. The members of the party addressed her as Durga Bhabhi. Durga Bhabhi became a white *ma'am*, Bhagat Singh became her *Saheb* (white husband), and Raj Guru their servant. Calcutta Mail's departure from Lahore was at 6.00 A.M. So all the three reached the station at the fixed time. Bhagat Singh had upturned the collar of his overcoat. Since it was winter, nobody suspected anything. There was police all over the platform. Bhagat Singh carried the young child of Durga Bhabhi in his arms. He was walking with his face under cover of the child. He and Raj Guru carried loaded pistols in their pockets, so that they could use them if forced to face the police. The co-operation of Durga Bhabhi with her child was a great sacrifice, an act of highly appreciable courage in such a grim situation. Howsoever profusely we praise her for this, it would still be less. These people bought first class tickets and boarded a first class compartment and befooling the police left for Calcutta.

As already reported, Chandra Shekhar Azad was an expert in disguising himself. So with a few of his friends, he formed a *toli* of the *Pandas* of Mathura (a group of *sadhus* who sing hymns and play on native musical instruments), and himself became their *guru* (head). With sandal mark on forehead, a stole (bearing the names Ram Ram) thrown over shoulders, a copy of the *Geeta* in hand, and singing hymns they also boarded the second class compartment of the same train and reached Lucknow. The dragnet of the police was still in place of course, with no results.

Manmath Nath Gupta gives a brief description of this event in the following words:

"In a very short time the police in the whole of Punjab became alert and the dogs of imperialism moved about scenting. Bhagat Singh, Raj Guru and Azad, though out of the compound of D.A.V. College, were still in Lahore, and Lahore had grown very hot. Bhagat Singh got himself a hair cut, and it is said that with Durga Devi and her baby Shachi he travelled in 1st class with aristocratic aplomb. Raj Guru became his orderly. Chandra Shekhar Azad, forming a group of pilgrims, left Lahore with them in the disguise of a *panda*."

In some books we come across this mention that Bhagat Singh disguised as *saheb* and Azad as a *ma'am*, but it appears difficult to believe. The reason is that it is simply ridiculous to imagine a man of Azad's strong and powerful dimensions disguising as a *ma'am*. Such a physique, however well you hide it, will tell its story itself: I am a man, not woman. Therefore it appears relevant that Durga Bhabhi herself posed as a *ma'am*. Most of the books give this version and this is considered right.

Some books mention that Raj Guru and Azad left train at Amritsar, but according to others they got down in Lucknow. Whatever the case, they successfully came out of Lahore.

Bhagat Singh went to Calcutta after this and worked covertly for the party from there. For about four and a half months ostensibly the activities of this party were stopped. It was essential to act like this, because due to the murder of Saunders the police was acting very cautiously.

Explosion in the Assembly

After despatching Saunders to *yamalok* (the abode of the dead), during his brief stay in Calcutta, Bhagat Singh came in contact with revolutionaries expert in making bombs, and with their cooperation he started the bomb manufacturing facilities in United Provinces and Punjab, and the manufacture of bombs started.

The central committee of 'Hindustan Samajwadi Ganatantrik Sena' decided that a bomb should be thrown in the Central Assembly. But its aim was to demonstrate opposition against the government, not to kill anybody. The members charged with causing the explosion of the bomb were clearly told that the bomb should be thrown at a place where it did not harm anybody. Besides, these bombs were simple and crude, and did not hurt anybody. Chandra Shekhar Azad, Bhagat Singh and many other members of the party cherished such a desire since long. After this decision, Bhagat Singh was supposed not to be associated with its execution, as the police was intensely searching him in the Saunders murder case. Bhagat Singh was not present when this decision was taken. But when he came to know of the decision, he was adamant. He said that this work should be entrusted to him alone. Chandra Shekhar did not want this. He reasoned with Bhagat Singh long and in detail, but Bhagat Singh did not budge. The central committee of the party again with a majority decision endorsed the name of Bhagat Singh, because he was considered the most suitable person for this job. Azad had to accept the majority decision.

After this the outlines of the plan were drawn. Chandra Shekhar Azad was of the opinion that after the bomb explosion, the revolutionaries should run away from the scene. He had visited the Assembly also with this in mind. He was convinced after a thorough inspection that running away from the Assembly was not difficult. For this he had drawn a map also as to from where they would run away, and where the motor to carry them would be stationed, but Bhagat Singh's opinion was totally different from it. He did not want that they ran away. Rather being arrested was a better option. His logic was that after arrest only the ideas of the party could be conveyed to the common public in the country and abroad, because in the court their stance could be publicly stated. Finally, Bhagat Singh's opinion was accepted. According to the description by Manmath Nath Gupta, Sukh Dev had advised Bhagat Singh for this course of action. In the opinion of Sukh Dev, only Bhagat Singh was capable of presenting the ideals and objectives of the party before the court in the best possible manner:

"He said that only Bhagat Singh, after his arrest, could present well the principles, ideals, objectives and the political implications of the bomb explosion from the stage of the court. In this context, even before the meeting of the central committee, he had urged Bhagat Singh to do it himself. When he could not persuade other members about his opinion, he separately talked to Bhagat Singh. He asked Bhagat Singh, why he allowed the central committee to take the decision that someone other than Bhagat Singh would go to throw bomb in the Assembly when he knew that no other person was capable of presenting the objectives of the party before the public?"

It should be remembered that earlier the names of Batukeshwar Dutt and Vijay Kumar Sinha were decided upon, for exploding bomb. Bhagat Singh felt disappointed with the following words of Batukeshwar Dutt and he told Dutt that much:

"Only I will go to explode bomb in the Assembly. The central committee will have to accept what I say. I will not reply to your insulting me. Please do not talk to me after this."

Batukeshwar Dutt was designed as an associate of Bhagat Singh in the task of bomb explosion.

Azad's name was not suggested by any member because in the opinion of all the members of the party it was only proper that he did not take part in such activities in the interest of the future of the party.

Two bills were tabled in the Central Assembly—the Public Safety Bill and the Industrial Disputes Bill. The objective of the first bill was to crush political movements, and that of the second to deprive workers the right to strike. So, these bills had become matters of dispute. People believed that even if the Assembly rejected these bills, the government would pass them under special power of the Viceroy.

On 8th April, 1929 the decision on these two bills was to be announced in the Assembly. Passes for Bhagat Singh and Batukeshwar Dutt were made on the recommendation of a nominated member of the Assembly. Both of them were wearing Khaki shirts and knickers. Jai Dev Kapoor got them seated at a proper place in the Assembly, so that they did not experience any inconvenience in throwing the bomb, and none was hurt.

The proceedings of the Assembly began. There was very strong opposition to the Public Safety Bill. The second, the Industrial Disputes Bill had been passed. (Different books give different accounts regarding this. We have reported the situation in concurrence with the opinion of Manmath Nath

Gupta. But according to some other books the Assembly had rejected both the Bills, only a declaration was to be made regarding their passage under the special rights of the Viceroy). As the speaker rose from his seat to make an announcement, Bhagat Singh and Batukeshwar Dutt rose in their seats. Bhagat Singh lobbed the bomb at the empty space behind the treasury benches. It was a terrible explosion. Everyone was taken aback. Before they could figure out anything the second bomb was also exploded. This scared people mortally, and they were shocked beyond comprehension. Sir George Schuster hid himself under a table. He injured himself a little bit in the scramble. The entire hall was filled with blue smoke. Both of them raised slogans—'Long Live the Revolution' and 'Down with Imperialism'—and threw pamphlets, which bore:

"One has to raise one's voice to make the deaf hear . Can we justify the propriety of our actions with these immortal words uttered on a similar occasion by Vellane, the anarchist martyr of France?

"We do not want to repeat the condemnable story of abominable insult which the British government has heaped upon our country during the last ten years in the name of reforms. We do not wish even to mention various insults tossed at our national leaders by this Assembly, which is known as Parliament also.

"We want to make it clear that there are some people who are hoping to get left over crumbs in the name of the Simon Commission, and others who are squabbling over the possibility of fresh bones. At this time the government is also perpetrating repressive laws on the public, like the Public Safety Act and the Industrial Disputes Act. Along with these the Press Sedition Act has been reserved for the next session of the Assembly. The labour leaders were earlier doing their work freely. Their indiscriminate arrests are making it absolutely clear what the intentions of the government are.

"Taking cognisance of these horribly provocative conditions and seriously realising its responsibilities the 'Hindustan Samajwadi Ganatantrik Sena' has ordered its army to commit the present act so that the insulting parody of law is stopped. May be the exploitative bureaucracy of the alien government is free to do what it likes, but it is absolutely essential to expose its naked form before the people.

"The elected representatives of the people should return to their constituencies, and prepare people for the revolution in the making. The government should realise that we oppose the Public Safety Act, the Industrial Disputes Act and the brutal murder of Lalaji, on behalf of the helpless people of India. We want to emphasise that it is easy to murder a man (and history is replete with examples) but you cannot murder ideas. Big empires have been cast in dustbins of history, but ideas have lived on. The Bruvan of France and the Czars of Russia have been destroyed but the revolutionaries have marched ahead with success of triumph.

"We consider human life sacred. We believe in such a bright future in which every human being will enjoy total peace and freedom. We are unhappy at our helplessness to shed human blood. But sacrifice of human beings is necessary for revolution. Long Live Revolution."

The pamphlet was issued on behalf of the Commander-in-Chief of the party. The name 'Balraj' appeared against the signatory.

Shri Manmath Nath Gupta has described this event in these words:

"The incident relates to 8th April, 1929. In the Central Assembly on the day a bill titled the Public Safety Bill was presented for consideration. There was a tug of war on both-sides. The 'Trade Disputes Bill' had been carried by a majority vote and the speaker Patel was readying himself to announce his decision on the 'Public Safety Bill'. All eyes were fixed on him. There was unusual excitement. At this time suddenly a deadly bomb was thrown from the visitors' gallery. No sooner did it explode than a smoke of terror engulfed the whole Assembly. Some persons including Sir George Schuster and Sir Bamanji Dal sustained minor injuries. Two young men had thrown the bombs. The name of one was Sardar Bhagat Singh and that of the other Batukeshwar Dutt."

According to a pre-planned arrangement, both

youngmen offered themselves for arrest. After this a long drama of justice was played which culminated into the award of sentence of hanging to Bhagat Singh, Raj Guru and Batukeshwar Dutt, and sentences of various durations to other revolutionaries. These will be taken up subsequently.

Plan to Blow up the Viceroy's Special Train

After the arrest of Bhagat Singh and Batukeshwar Dutt, they were charged with the murder of Saunders and many members of their party had been arrested in connexion with this murder. So, the party in a sense lay in tatters. Azad was still the Commander of this party. He had all the traits, such as competence, courage and dedication, required for the post. Besides him, there were Bhagwati Charan Verma, his wife Durga Devi, Sushila Didi, Shri Yash Pal et al. So the activities of the party continued.

A plan to blow up the special train of the Viceroy was chalked out as a aprt of these activities. First, 27th October, 1929 was fixed for this. But then it could not be executed that day for some unavoidable reasons. Later on, 23rd December, 1929 was fixed.

They had to prepare long for this work. One member of the party was despatched to Nizamuddin railway station to observe the situation in the guise of a *sadhu.* That day the Viceroy's special was scheduled to arrive at Delhi from Kolhapur. A few days earlier the bombs were carefully planted below the railway track. These bombs were connected to a battery a few hundred yards away. They could be detonated from the distance with a switch. For many days the trains continued to pass from over them without harm to anybody. When Viceroy's special passed from over it, the switch was pressed on. It resulted into a terrible explosion. However, to his good luck the Viceroy was saved. It was late by a few seconds. As a result the Viceroy was clean saved, but the third boggy following his was completely blown off.

This incident caused a stir again. The police was already alert. Now it was flabbergasted. It intensified its activities all the more.

In 1930 in the Lahore session of the Congress, whereas

on one side for the first time complete freedom was demanded, on the other this incident was condemned. Main extract of the resolution ran like this:

"This Congress condemns the action of the bomb explosion on the Viceroy's special, and again reiterates its definite view that such activities are not only opposed to the objectives of the Congress, they harm national interests as well. This Congress felicitates His Excellency the Viceroy, Lady Irwin and their other companions along with humble servants for their lucky hair-breadth escape."

In spite of the failure of the attempt to blow up the Viceroy special, the party was active under Chandra Shekhar Azad's leadership. Bomb explosions, dacoities and murders were planned many times for many occasions, but they did not yield any noteworthy success. The police continued to chase like hell to arrest the members of this party. Roop Chand, Inder Pal, Jehangir La and Kundan La.—4 members of this party were arrested in 1930. After this some more members of the party were arrested. In all the police arrested 26 persons. But it could not lay its hands on Chandra Shekhar Azad, the president of the party, Yash Pal, Sushila Didi, Durga Bhabhi, Hans Raj, Prakash Vati etc. So, they were declared absconders.

The police could not arrest Sukhdev Raj also. The police informers were roaming here and there in search of the absconding accused. One day the police came to know that Sukhdev Raj was in the Shalimar Park in Lahore along with one young man. The police surrounded the area. It did not get any trace of Sukhdev Raj. However, a young man, named Jagdish Raj, in the course of his struggle died of police firing.

The arrested persons were awarded different sentences in the cases against them. Initially, Gulab Singh, Jehangir Lal and Amrik Singh were awarded death sentences. Later on Amrik Singh was acquitted and the other two were deported. Other accused were awarded varied sentences.

7
Travesty of Justice and Azad

The path of revolution is not a bed of roses, it is razor's edge. Every wayfarer of this path knows this harsh truth. So it is not given to a common man to traverse this path. Only a few honest and courageous men are competent to go this way. The truth is that a rare brave soul, prepared to die any moment, can adopt this path. The revolutionaries such as Chandra Shekhar Azad and his ilk were such brave souls.

The Case of the Assembly Bomb Explosion

Azad had carved out a special status for himself in the party right from the initial revolutionary period in 'Hindustan Samajwadi Ganatantrik Association'. He was nicknamed as 'Quick Silver' (mercury) in the party for his indomitable courage and unusual caution. Azad proved himself worthy of this name throughout his revolutionary life. He took part in so many events. The police was using every resource at its disposal. But it is not possible to catch or hold mercury in hand. He was destined not to be caught. And he was not caught.

Bhagat Singh and Batukeshwar Dutt had got themselves arrested after the explosion in the Assembly. As a result, after arrest they were taken to the police station, Chandni Chowk. Here they refused to make any statement, because they wanted to make a statement in the court only. After this, they were kept in the lockup in civil line police station. Sardar Kishan Singh, the father of Bhagat Singh, came to meet him. But he was not allowed.

On 22nd April, 1929 he was shifted from the police lockup to Delhi jail. Sardar Kishan Singh met him on 3rd May along with his advocate, Asif Ali. Though Sardar Kishan Singh wanted to contest the case with all strength and legal support, Bhagat Singh was opposed to it from the view point of defending himself.

The case started on 7th May, 1929 in the court of the additional magistrate, Mr. Tool. The court had its sittings in the jail itself. When the government had presented its version, Bhagat Singh and Batukeshwar Dutt were asked to make their statements, but they refused to make a statement saying "We shall depose before the court of the sessions judge." So the case was sent to the court of the sessions judge, Middleton. This court also had its sittings in the jail, and the hearing in the case began from 4th June, 1929. Bhagat Singh made his famous historic statement. His statement sheds bright light on the objectives of the party. Some extracts are produced here below:

"We have been charged with serious crimes. We want to present an explanation of our conduct. The following questions come up in this context:

1. Whether the bombs were thrown in the Assembly? If yes, what was the reason there of?

2. Whether the charges framed by the lower court are correct or not?

"We admit the first half of the first question, but some of our friends have given an incorrect version of the incident. We admit the responsibility for throwing the bomb. We, therefore, expect that our statement would be taken and evaluated in correct perspective. For example, we want to point out that the averment 'They snatched a pistol from the hand of one of us' is a deliberate lie. In fact, when we surrendered ourselves, neither of us had a pistol in his hand. Some of our friends have not hesitated in uttering a white lie who have said that they saw us throwing the bomb. We expect that the people whose objective is to maintain the purity and impartiality of justice will themselves draw their own conclusion from facts.

"We will have to elaborate in detail in reply to the second half of the first question so that we may fully and openly explain those objectives and situations due to which this incident took place, an incident which has assumed a historic dimension now. In jail some police officers met us. When some of them told us that after the incident under consideration, Lord Irwin, in the course of his address to the joint session of both the houses of the Assembly, had observed that by throwing the bomb we had not attacked a person as such but the constitution itself, then it appeared to us that a correct evaluation of the incident had not been made.

"We love mankind no less than others. Therefore, there is hardly a question of our being jealous of anybody. On the contrary, in our eyes, human life is so sacred that it cannot be described in words.

"Our aim was to express our practical opposition to an institution which had demonstrated in a crass form right from its beginning not only its uselessness but long-lasting harmful power also. The more we thought about it the more we arrived at this conclusion that the objective of the existence of this institution (Assembly) was to demonstrate to the world the poverty and helplessness of India, and that it had become a symbol of irresponsible, autocratic and repressive power.

"The demands of the representatives of the public are being thrown into the dustbin. The pious resolutions passed by the house are trampled over in an insulting manner by the so-called Indian Parliament. The resolutions relating to the stoppage of repressive and autocratic laws are treated with the highest disdainful indifference, and the government has unilaterally accepted those resolutions and laws which have been rejected by the representatives of the public.

"In short, in spite of making all sincere efforts we fail to understand how the existence of an institution can be justified, whose glory and grandeur is being maintained by spending the hard earned money of crores of Indians, even though it has been reduced to a meaningless and satanic conspiracy only.

"Thus we fail to understand the justification of the thinking of those leaders who are wasting the time and money of public in a preplanned demonstration of helpless slavery of India. We have been thinking seriously on this issue and the mass arrest of labour leaders on presentation of the

 Chandra Shekhar Azad : An Immortal Revolutionary of India

Industrial Disputes Bill, and when we came to the Assembly to have a first hand information of the dispute being raised about it, our thinking was all the more confirmed that the crores of Indian workers could not get anything from an institution which had reduced itself to a horrific memorial of the strangulating exploiters and slavery of the helpless workers.

"The representatives of the entire country have been insulted in such a manner that we call it inhuman and barbaric. In addition to this, crores of hungry and poor people have been deprived of their basic resource of fundamental rights and financial interests.

"No person, who has a sympathy like ours for the miserable condition of the mute and helpless workers, can be a silent spectator to all this. Nor will those keep quiet who have an abiding love for the work as who have given their sweat and blood in the formation of financial structure for the exploiters who find a major support in this government. No one can suppress the heartrending voice (of millions), sent out by a churning in the soul caused by callous exploitation. Consequently, we have drawn inspiration from those words of late Shri C.R. Das, former member (law) of the executive council of the Governor General, which he wrote in a letter to his son, to the effect that England needed a bomb to rise from its nightmare. And we have thrown a bomb on the floor of the Assembly on behalf of those millions who were left with no other option to give vent to their heart-rending suffering. Our sole objective was to make our voice heard by the deaf, and communicate the writing on the wall to those who are not seeing it. We have warned those people who are ceaselessly rushing ahead unmindful of the impending doom.

"We have used the words 'imaginary non-violence' earlier in the context. We want to explain it. According to our point of view the use of force is unjust when it is used in an aggressive manner. According to us it is violence. But when force is used for a specified purpose, then it is morally just. Total exclusion of the use of force is a blank illusion only. A new movement is coming up in this country and we have already made it known. This movement draws its inspiration from the actions of Guru Govind Singh, Shivaji, Kamal Pasha and Riza Khan, Washington and Garibaldi, La Fayetc and Lenin.

"We formed an impression that the alien government and the political leaders of India had closed their eyes to this movement and their ears have not heard its voice. Therefore, we deemed it our duty to warn at such places where our voice would not remain unheard. We had no personal jealousy or enmity against those people who suffered minor injuries during the incident. We deliberately threw the bomb in the Assembly. The facts are themselves clear. We urge that our objective should be evaluated on the basis of results of our actions, and not based on imaginary situations and prejudices. Despite the proofs submitted by the government experts the fact remains that only one empty bench has been damaged and less than one dozen people have suffered minor scratches from the bombs we threw in the Assembly. The scientists of the government have called it a miracle, but in our eyes it is just a scientific process. The first point is that the bombs exploded between empty benches and desks, and the second point is this: The persons, such as Shiv Rao, Shiv Shankar Rao and Mr. George Schuster, who were just two feet away from the site of explosion, either did not suffer any injury or received just scratches. Had the bombs been stuffed with powerful elements such as potassium chlorate and picrite, they would have pierced through impediments and obstacles and hurt people sitting far away. Had they been stuffed with still more powerful elements, they could have killed a majority of the members of the Assembly. We could do this also that we threw them at the treasury boxes where important people sat. Finally, we could do this as well that we hit Sir John Simon, who was sitting in the speaker's gallery, and whose unfortunate commission was hated by every intelligent individual in the country."

Earlier, appearing before the court, Bhagat Singh explaining the meaning of 'revolution' had said:

"Revolution allows no room for lethal weapons. Neither does it offer scope for taking personal revenge. Revolution is not the culture of bombs and revenge. What we mean by 'revolution' is that an order based on injustice should change.

Even though the exploiters deprive them of the fruits of their labour and fundamental rights, the workers and producers are an essential part of society. On one side the farmers, who produce foodgrains for all, are dying of hunger. The weavers do not find clothes for themselves and their families, even though they supply clothes to all the markets of the world. Likewise the blacksmiths, carpenters and other workers in construction industry build palatial buildings for others, and yet they are condemned to live in slums and dirty localities. On the other hand, capitalists, exploiters and others, living like parasites and leeches, waste crores of rupees to satisfy their crazes. These horrible inconsistencies and inartificial equalities in the opportunities for development are driving the society towards anarchy.

"If these are ignored, then the present administrative order will block the road of newly rising natural forces, and if this order continues then it is definite that a serious struggle will ensue, which will result in throwing away all impeding elements and the havenots will dominate to realise the objectives of revolution. Revolution is the birthright of mankind. Freedom is such a birthright of men that it cannot be snatched away. Labour class form the true basis of society. The ultimate aim of the workers is the establishment of the sovereignty of the people. We shall undergo all the pains and suffering handed out to us by this court to uphold this faith and these ideals. We are determined to offer our young age to burn as an incense on this altar. No sacrifice is too big for this great objective. We shall patiently wait for the growth and spread of the revolution. Long Live Revolution."

This statement naturally drew the attention of the country towards him and his party. He did not make any attempt to defend himself in this case. The court proceedings in this case were complete by 10th June, 1929, and two days later on 12th June the judgement was read out, in which both Bhagat Singh and Batukeshwar Dutt were sentenced for life imprisonment. After this Bhagat Singh was sent to Mianwali, the notorious jail of Punjab and Batukeshwar Dutt to Lahore Central Jail.

Bhagat Singh knew that the attempts to defend himself would not yield any results, so he did not attempt any self-defence. The aim of his above statement was only this that the people knew his thoughts. He preferred an appeal in the Punjab High Court to further publicise his objectives among people.

The appeal came up for hearing before Justice Ford and Justice Edison in the high court in Lahore. Here also Bhagat Singh made a statement highlighting his objectives. He tried to prove through his statement that he was not a criminal but that he was a warrior struggling for the freedom of his motherland. He particularly emphasised that an accused should be awarded a punishment keeping in mind the objectives of his action:

"Unless the feelings of an accused are known, one can not know his real objectives. If the objective is completely forgotten, then no justice is dispensed to a person. In the event of ignoring the objectives, even the highest commanders would look like ordinary murderers. Most of the government tax collectors would appear thieves and forgerers, and even judges would be charged with murders. This will reduce the social order and culture to bloodshed, thievery and forgery. In the event of ignoring the objectives, what right would the government have in expecting a fair play and justice from the individuals in society? If the objective is ignored, then every religious preaching would appear as preaching of lies and every prophet would be charged with misleading crores of ignorant and innocent people. If objectives are ignored and forgotten, then Lord Jesus Christ would be considered a man who created disturbances, breached peace and spread rebellion, and would be treated as a dangerous person in terms of law, but we worship Him and carry unlimited respect for Him in our hearts."

Lahore High Court dismissed the appeal and upheld the judgement of the lower court. In Jail, Bhagat Singh started a fast unto death on 15th June, 1929 in support of facilities for political prisoners. On receiving this news, Batukeshwar Dutt also started hunger strike on that very day in Lahore Central Jail in his support. Bhagat Singh was alone in Mianwali Jail. Now a case on account of murder of Saunders was also to be instituted against him. Other accused in this case of murder were in Lahore Central Jail. So he made an application to the Inspector General Jails, Punjab State for his transfer to Lahore Central Jail. His request was accepted, and he was sent to Lahore Central Jail in the last week of this month itself.

Case of the Lahore Kand (Saunders' Murder)

The case in Saunders' murder *kand*, which is known as the Lahore *kand* also, started on 10th July, 1929 in Lahore in the court of magistrate Shri Krishna. Bhagat Singh and Batukeshwar Dutt were on hunger strike. So, they were brought to court on stretcher. After this the other accused also started hunger strike in their support. On 14th July, 1929 Bhagat Singh sent a letter to the member Home Deptt., Government of India, in which he demanded facilities for the prisoners. The government did not attach any importance to these demands, so the strike continued. The health of the prisoners deteriorated day by day. Bhagat Singh's weight, who weighed 133 pounds in the beginning, continued dropping at the rate of 5 pounds per week. It stabilised after some time.

Death of Jatin Das Due to Fast unto Death

As a consequence of hunger strike the condition of Jatin Das (Yatindra Nath Das) continued deteriorating by the day. It caused a big stir in the country. He was constantly advancing towards death. Leaders like Motilal Nehru and Jawahar Lal Nehru raised their voice on this issue through the medium of newspapers. Other leaders such as Dr. Gopi Nath Bhargava and Purushottam Das Tandon came to see them in jail. They made their best efforts to save the life of Jatin Das by persuading him to give up hunger strike, but did not meet with success. After meeting Jatin Das, Pandit Jawahar La Nehru described his critical condition in the following words:

"The condition of Yatindra Das has grown very critical. He has become unusually weak. He does not have the strength to change sides. He speaks very slowly and slowly. In fact, he is advancing towards his death. I felt great pain on seeing the suffering of these brave young men. It appears that they have joined this battle by putting their life at stake.

They want that the political prisoners should be treated as political prisoners. am fully confident that this *tapasya* (sacrifice) is destined to be crowned with success."

Hunger strike was resorted to in many other jails in support of Jatin Das. Due to this hunger strike the dates in the case were also advanced and postponed. Later on the Punjab jail committee formed a sub-committee to consider these demands for reforms. So, on 2nd September, 1929, barring Jatin Das all others gave up hunger strike. This sub-committee recommended the release also of Jatin Das. But the government did not agree to release him without bail bond. And Jatin Das refused to sign his bail-bond. Seeing the serious condition of Jatin Das, many others including Bhagat Singh started hunger strike again. Ultimately, on 13th September, 1929 Jatin Das passed away at 1.05 P.M. Netaji Subhash Chandra Bose arranged and remitted rupees six hundred to get his dead body sent to Calcutta. So, his dead body was sent to Calcutta, where lakhs of people paid their tributes to him on his last rites.

Case Transferred to a Judicial Tribunal

On 1st May, 1930 through a special ordinance this case was transferred to a judicial tribunal. It consisted of three judges, appointed by the Chief Justice of Lahore High Court. This judicial tribunal was empowered to carry on the court proceedings even if the accused were not present.

This tribunal started the hearing in the case on 5th May from Poonch House, Lahore. These accused sang songs of patriotism. They believed that all the legal proceedings were a farce. So they adopted dilatory tactics in every court proceeding. Once in the backdrop of one such incident, the chairman of the tribunal, Justice Cold Stream, ordered the police to beat the accused with shoes and lathis. So the accused started boycotting the proceedings of the court from the next day and demanded that Justice Cold Stream be transferred. On this day the accused were maltreated by the police. The Indian member of the tribunal, Justice Haider Agha, also criticised this step. So along with Justice Cold Stream, Justice Haider Agha was also transferred, and a new tribunal consisting of Justice G.C. Hilton, Justice Abdul

Quadir and Justice J.K. Tap was constituted.

The accused continued with their boycott of the court. Bhagat Singh said that Justice Cold Stream should apologise for his conduct. The government sent Justice Cold Stream on a long leave. How else could the government accept the demand of Bhagat Singh?

Judgement

Proceedings were carried on one-sided in the absence of the accused in the tribunal. The court completed its work by 26th August, 1930. Then a message was sent to the accused that they were invited to say, if they so wanted, something themselves in their self defence or through a lawyer or present a witness. The accused understood well the meaning of this whole exercise (drama); since, after the completion of the whole proceedings, only the judgement was awaited, they rejected it.

On 7th October, 1930, the judgement in the case was pronounced. Since the accused had boycotted the court, a special messenger came to the jail and read it out to them.

According to the judgement, the accused were awarded the following sentences:

Sentence to death: Bhagat Singh, Raj Guru and Sukh Dev.

Deportation: Kamal Nath Tiwari, Jai Dev Kapoor, Vijay Kumar Sinha, Shiv Verma, Gaya Prasad, Mahavir Singh, and Kishori Lal.

Seven years' imprisonment: Kundan Lal

Three years' imprisonment: Prem Das.

Others, such as Jitendra Sanyal, Master Asha Ram, Ajay Ghosh, Desh Raj and Surendra Nath Pandey were let off.

After the Judgement

Immediately after the judgement by the court, section 144 was invoked in Lahore which banned holding of any kind of demonstration, or meeting or pasting posters in the city. In spite of all these precautions observed by the administration, on the same evening a vast rally was held in the Municipal Maidan without any prior notice, in which the entire legal proceedings were criticised. It is surprising that in spite of a very strict vigil in jail, the journalists succeeded in taking the photographs of Bhagat Singh and his companions, which they published in their papers along with their articles.

The whole country was flooded with demonstrations, and strikes in protest of these sentences. Some students and a professor of D.A.V. College attacked the police. A strike was held on 8th October on a call given by the students union. Most of the teaching institutions remained closed voluntarily. This was reflected all over India.

Bhagat Singh's father submitted a letter to the governor in which he requested for giving an opportunity to prove that on the day of Saunders' murder Bhagat Singh was in Calcutta. But Bhagat Singh publicly opposed this action of his father. An appeal was submitted to the privy council. Mahamana Madan Mohan Malviya put in an appeal for mercy to the governor. People from all over the country raised their voice to get this sentence changed; people sent memoranda, supported by mass signatures, to the governor, but the result of all this was zero. And on 23rd March, 1931 all the three brave were executed in Lahore jail.

The country's anger did not lose its fury even after the executions. The newspapers all over the country condemned this action of the government. Mahatma Gandhi overshadowed the Indian politics at this time. In February, 1931 he struck a deal with the Viceroy, Lord Irwin, which is known as the Gandhi-Irwin agreement. The Indian public was waiting for the publication of the report of this agreement with great expectations. The public fully believed that Gandhiji would definitely save these brave sons of India from hanging. But when the report came out, all their expectations were watered down. There was no mention of this issue in the agreement. Yes, all the Congress *satyagrahis*, who were in jails were announced to be released. This action of Gandhiji was intensely and extensively criticised. The journalists put questions to him on this issue at different places. Just a few days later after these hangings when Gandhiji came to Karachi to attend the Congress session, he was shown black flags.

Meetings were held in different places in Punjab after these hangings. People took oaths by writing in blood to take revenge. The farmers stopped paying revenue. Bhagat Singh had become like an *Aradhya Dev* (a god for worship) to them. Their pictures sold like hot cakes. Biographical books dealing with the courageous saga of these braves began publishing all over the country. The government considered these books a shadow of death for itself. As a consequence, these books and photos were banned.

After the martyrdom of these braves one chapter of the history of Indian revolutionaries came to an end.

Azad's Role During This Period

Azad did not sit idle after the arrest of Bhagat Singh and others. He was doing something or the other. The efforts to blow up the Viceroy special confirms this. Besides, he met Pandit Motilal Nehru and his son Jawahar La Nehru also. Though there was a difference between his principles and those of the Congress, both had common objectives. He had very cordial relations with the Nehru family. Though this family did not openly support the revolutionaries, yet it had deep sympathy with these brave persons. It is said that during this period when he was at large, he visited *Anand Bhavan* in Allahabad in 1930. He met Pandit Motilal Nehru here. Pandit Nehru is presumed to have advised him to give up violence which Azad rejected in humble words. He said that he did not believe in non-violence, and he was not sure that the Britishers would quit India in pursuance of the policy of non-violence of the Congress. He considered violence essential to throw the Britishers out. Later on he met Jawahar La Nehru also. There was an award of rupees ten thousand on his arrest, and he was moving about so freely. Jawahar La Nehru was greatly surprised at this. He advised Azad to remain cautious in this regard. But Azad could not care less. He said only this that the police could not catch him alive. During this period it was also circulated that talks of some kind of agreement were going on between Gandhiji and Lord Irwin. In this context Azad had asked Nehruji what was being proposed in this agreement for the revolutionaries who risked their lives every moment. Possibly Pandit Nehru did not reply to this question because he knew that even after this agreement it would not be possible to save these brave souls. He knew Gandhiji would talk to Irwin, but loved his principles the most. But it was Nehru's most cordial desire that these revolutionaries should be saved. Expressing the pain he suffered after the hanging of Bhagat Singh and others, Nehru said:

"I kept quiet during the last days of Bhagat Singh and his compatriots, because I knew that my speaking might jeopardise the possibility of cancellation of his sentence to death by hanging. I kept quiet, whereas I desired that I burst out. All of us could not save them through our combined efforts also, who were so dear to us, and whose great sacrifice and great courage was a source of inspiration to young men, and still is. People will express regret in the country on our helplessness, but at the same time our country is proud of this heavenly soul, and when England talks to us for agreement, then we should not forget the dead body of Bhagat Singh."

One informer, Kailash Pati, mentioned the name of Jawahar La Nehru also to police just because Nehru carried sympathies for the revolutionaries deep in his heart. Manmath Nath Gupta, in this context, writes:

"His memory was marvellous. In his statement he named scores of people from Lahore to Calcutta. The tempo with which he assumed the role of a revolutionary, with the same tempo he turned informer. He cared for nothing then, nothing now. If he involved Pandit Jawahar Lal Nehru in his statement, then who else could be spared?"

It is clear that though Nehruji had full sympathy for the revolutionaries, he found himself helpless in doing something for them.

Azad's Efforts for the Release of Bhagat Singh

In 1930 the movement of the Congress was on upswing, and, therefore, the revolutionary party also decided to step its activities. At this time Bhagat Singh and many other members of the party were in jail. But Azad was not sitting idle. He had Shri Bhagwati Charan as his main associate. He was convinced that the government was definitely going to hang Bhagat Singh. Azad and Bhagwati Charan thought of drawing a plan for Bhagat Singh's escape from jail. They considered the various aspects of the plan. The government was hell bent on hanging Bhagat Singh. If he could be freed from jail at this time, it would have created a stir world-wide. Azad wanted to shake the government to its foundations by executing this plan.

Azad and Bhagwati Charan thought for many days about the plan as to how much preparation would be required. Since it would involve the death of a number of policemen and members of the party, bombs and pistols were also required for it. They needed a car or two to car y all this material, and a house on rent near the jail to hide all the weapons. It was also considered if some women were to be involved in the plan or not. Once the plan got its final shape, Yash Pal, Sukh Dev Raj, Dhanwantari and others were informed about it and it was decided that the cooperation would be sought from Durga Devi and Sushila Devi.

A house on Bahawalpur Road of Lahore was taken on rent. The above named two lady members started living there so that none entertained any suspicion regarding as to who lived there. People in the neighbourhood thought that a family lived there.

1st June, 1930 was fixed for it. Bhagat Singh and Batukeshwar Dutt were in Lahore central jail, and the other accused of the Lahore *Kand* were in Borstal jail. Since the case was one, therefore the government had agreed to allow all the accused to meet once a week on Sundays, so that they could exchange views among themselves. On that day Bhagat Singh and Dutt were to be taken from central jail to Borstal jail for the whole day. It was decided that when the police took Bhagat Singh and Batukeshwar Dutt out of the jail gate, and would be escorting them to the police van parked at some distance, then they would swoop upon the police with bombs and revolvers, and would keep their car ready at a proper place. When the police and the revolutionaries would be engaged with one another, then Bhagat Singh and Batukeshwar Dutt would sit in that car and the driver would take them away. Two groups of revolutionaries were formed to swoop upon the police. One group, led by Bhagwati Charan, would attack the police with bombs, while the other group, led by Chandra Shekhar Azad, would stop with revolvers the chasing police.

Bhagat Singh, too, was contacted and his advice taken in respect of this plan. The security arrangement of the police at Borstal jail was comparatively less than at the central jail. So Bhagat Singh thought that it would be better if the police was attacked outside Borstal jail. But Borstal jail was on the backside, some distance away from the main road. So, there was a possibility of the central jail police arriving there while Bhagat Singh and Batukeshwar Dutt were trying to get into the car, and they had to face it again second time. Finally it was settled that the police would be swooped upon outside the central jail. The plan was exciting. It was definite that a few persons on both sides would definitely be killed. But the revolutionaries had never feared death. They devoted themselves, heart and soul, to execute it. Bhagat Singh and Dutt were properly informed.

Death of Bhagwati Charan

Bombs were made for this plan. Bhagwati Charan decided to test them in advance in order to ascertain their utility. 28th May was fixed for testing. He along with two more revolutionaries, Sukh Dev Raj and Bachchan, reached the banks of Ravi, and then crossing it went into the forests.

Other revolutionaries were staying in the Bahawalpur Road house. There were just two days left to implement the plan. So the other persons, present there, got busy with the cleaning, oiling of weapons. Azad had assigned fixed, separate responsibilities to each one of them. Now they were doing their work. In the meanwhile, they saw wounded Sukh Dev Raj coming in a tonga. He was crying with pain. He had his leg dressed in cotton which had turned red due to excessive bleeding from the wound. He was taken down from tonga, and then taken in. They learnt from him that during examination the bomb exploded in his hand, blowing it away. It caused serious injury to the leg of Sukh Dev Raj also. The condition of Bhagwati Charan was very serious. He sent Sukh Dev back here to inform other members of the incident. Describing the incident, Veerendra writes:

"Sukh Dev Raj did not want to leave him. But Bhagwati Charan said, 'There is no hope of surviving. There has been so much bleeding that I cannot be saved now. Neither can you take me to Bahawalpur Road house. I do not want this also that some persons start doubting if they saw me in this form, and this spelt some trouble to my comrades. Therefore, you leave me here and go and ask others to be careful. Don't worry for me. I'll see what happens".

All the members felt unspeakable pain when they heard of this incident. The revolutionaries were not afraid of death. No one would have felt so pained if Bhagwati Charan died in the process of getting Bhagat Singh freed. No one had imagined that he would meet such a death.

No one could say whether he was alive or dead at that moment, when they learnt of it. So Yash Pal went to that place along with two-three young men to bring him from there. His condition was precarious. Death was imminent, just a few moments away. His last desire was to see Azad before passing away. Along with this he told Yash Pal that the plan to free Bhagat Singh should not be stopped or suspended. He was very unhappy till his last moment for not being unable to participate in it.

He was in throes of extreme pain and moaning. His condition deteriorated by the second. So, it was not possible to carry him from there on hands or shoulders. Leaving a comrade there with him, Yash Pal went towards the city to find a stretcher or a *charpoy*, and, if possible, to get a doctor for him. A few moments after Yash Pal left, Bhagwati Charan left this world.

Later at night when Yash Pal returned with a *charpoy*, sheets and medicine, he found Bhagwati Charan's dead body only. The comrade he had left behind to look after Bhagwati Charan ran away out of fear. Yash Pal felt highly disappointed and pained at this. The dead body was wrapped in the sheet. Leaving him alone there, Yash Pal came home to discuss with his companions. Everybody was plunged in sorrow on hearing the news of his death. Next morning Azad, Yash Pal and other two or three companions prepared themselves to go there. Durga Devi, the wife of Bhagwati Charan, also wanted to accompany them. But it was dangerous to carry a woman on bicycle to such a place. In this house, and under these conditions she could neither weep nor cry her heart out even at the loss of her husband. On this occasion, Chandra Shekhar wrote to her:

"You are our mother. Our sister. We alone can protect your honour, and you can protect ours. I can understand your feelings, but you and Bhagwati Bhai trampled over your feelings the day both of you joined this party. If you have already sacrificed so much, kindly sacrifice a little more."

So, Durga Devi could not see her husband for the last time. Azad and Yash Pal reached the place where the dead body of Bhagwati Charan was lying. It was buried in the ground, because it was very difficult to take it to a cremation ground. No vehicle could reach this place in the jungle. If they carried it, say, on shoulder, then the chances were that the police might have come to know of it, spelling serious trouble to all others.

This description is based on 'Vey Inqualabi Din', a book by Veerendra. Shri Manmath Nath Gupta has given a somewhat different version of Bhagwati Charan's death. According to him, Bhagwati Charan's entrails had come out in this incident. In his words:

'The death of Bhagwati Charan is a painful event in the history of revolution. Many types of things are heard in this regard. Only this much is undisputed in all that has been learnt that on 28th May, 1930 Bhagwati Charan went to the banks of Ravi river with a bomb at 4.30 p.m. with an intention to experiment. There the bomb exploded suddenly and he was seriously injured. It is said that the injury forced all his entrails to come out, and yet he was swearing by the party till the last. He survived for three or four hours, but the circumstances were such or caused in a manner that medical aid could not be rushed to him."

Undoubtedly, Bhagwati Charan's death was a big set-back to the revolutionary party and also to the plan to free Bhagat Singh.

Failure of the Plan

Though the death of Bhagwati Charan came as a big

shock to the party, the complete execution of the plan was a must. A strange vacuum was cast over the pervasive grieving sadness. None knew how to get over this emptiness. Durga Devi was in a state of strange shock. The poor lady could not weep. Neither she talked. So, Azad, being the leader of the party, had to take an initiative. He said to Durga Devi that as per the last wish of Bhagwati Charan, Bhagat Singh had to be freed. On this the brave lady said:

"Bhaiya! If you have to execute this work, I'll go with you in his place."

Every one was delighted with these words of Durga. But she had a four-year-old baby, and the execution of the plan called for putting life at stake. In the event of her being killed the child would have been totally orphaned. Seeing all this, the other lady, Sushila, offered herself as a substitute. Azad heard both of them, and as a leader of the party, he ordered:

"This is not the work of ladies. Neither of you two will go. Is it a small work which you are doing as of now? Now we will go and test our luck."

So on 1ˢᵗ June, 1930, according to the pre-fixed time, Azad, Yash Pal, Vaishampayan and two-three other young members left and reached near the central jail to achieve their objective. Everyone occupied his post, fully ready as per plan. Bhagat Singh was already informed about this plan. But it could not succeed.

Two opinions are available why this plan did not succeed. According to one opinion, the vehicle which would carry both the prisoners was parked on the road some distance away from the jail gate, and the prisoners had to walk this distance on foot, but on this day the vehicle was parked just next to the gate, and moved out from there, carrying the prisoners inside it. Chandra Shekhar Azad and others just stared, amazed.

The second opinion is different from this. According to this, at the last moment Bhagat Singh gave up the idea of running away from jail. Shri Veerendra has described this incident in line with this opinion. According to him:

"This was also a part of this plan, that when Bhagat Singh and Dutt would come out, Vaishampayan would play on his flute, and Bhagat Singh would scratch his head, which would mean that he was ready. Activity would start after this. But for a reason best known to Bhagat Singh, he did not pass on the hint. As soon as they came out of jail, he and Dutt sat in the prisoners' vehicle and the police escorted them away from there. Azad and his companions just watched in blank amazements. They could not understand as to what had happened. They returned disappointed.

After some time when Bhagat Singh was asked why he behaved the way he did, he replied that after the death of Bhagwati Charan he was left with no desire to live. He did not want this as well that Azad, the last symbol of the party, was killed in this attempt. Bhagat Singh did not desire his release at the cost of elimination of Azad. So when he came out of jail he saw that his companions were standing there. Even then he did not prepare himself for this activity. Who knows how many were killed in this exercise?"

Moments of Doubt

The failure of this plan caused immense suffering to Azad. When he reached his Bahawalpur Road house, he did not talk to anybody and went into a room. The most trusted companion of Azad was Bhagat Singh, and next to him was Bhagwati Charan. Bhagwati Charan had already left this world and the hanging noose was awaiting Bhagat Singh. Azad kept himself closed in the room for many hours, thinking about all this. It was an unusually trying time. On one side his closest friend was in jail, and a charade of justice was being staged to hang him. On the other hand the last wish of late Bhagwati Bhai was that Bhagat Singh should definitely be freed. Unfortunately the entire plan had flopped. What to do, and what not to do? That was the question staring him in his face. In the end, overcoming all his doubts, Azad decided to make one more attempt to free Bhagat Singh. He considered it cowardice to surrender, defeated by the circumstances.

Azad took this unwavering decision and went to sleep. But seemed luck did not favour him. In the night one of the bombs exploded by itself at home. The explosion shook the doors and windows and everybody woke up. Azad ordered everybody to clear out of the place carrying whatever one could lay his hands upon. There was a possibility of the police reaching there. In that event the situation would have turned unimaginably terrible. But another big problem was as to where the ladies could be taken. An engineer lived next to this house. Yash Pal went to him to avert the difficulty that he might inform the police. He narrated his entire story to the engineer and requested him not to inform the police of this explosion at least for half an hour. In the meanwhile all the revolutionaries would leave that place. Then the police could be informed. Respecting the feelings of the revolutionaries, the engineer agreed to this. So all the revolutionaries cleared safely out of that place.

Sukh Dev Raj was wounded, but it was not possible to admit him to any hospital. Dhanwantari found out a solution to this problem. Dr. Asanand, the principal of Dayanand Ayurvedic College, Lahore was a man of nationalistic views. Dhanwantari at sometime was his student also. Dr. Asanand kept Sukh Dev Raj at his home and took upon himself the responsibility of treating him. He operated on the leg of Sukh Dev Raj. His treatment resulted into fast recovery in the leg of Sukh Dev Raj. He was sent to Amritsar later on.

So, even after a series of failures, the foremost issue before Azad was to re-organise the party. This needed money. He left Lahore and reached Delhi to arrange money. Garodia Store dacoity, reffered to above, was committed by him at this time.

Yash Pal's Surveillance

Though the party did not object to its members to marry, however, it was expected of the active members that they stayed unmarried. If somebody wanted to marry, he had to seek permission of the party. After the Garodia Store dacoity, the party had started a factory in Delhi. Outwardly it was a factory for the manufacturing of soap and hair oil, but they manufactured picric acid used in the making of bombs, here. Shri Agyeya was the director of this factory. Besides Agyeya, many others like Kailash Pati, Vimla Prasad Jain, his wife, Yash Pal and Prakash Vati lived here. Yash Pal and Prakash Vati became very close. They were observed living together.

This was against the rules of the party. So, the party decided to shoot Yash Pal dead. This job was entrusted to Veer Bhadra Tiwari. Tiwari, instead of shooting him, broke this news to him. Yash Pal went into the factory with a revolver in hand and went to Lahore with Prakash Vati.

Later on Yash Pal married Prakash Vati. He met Azad afterwards. Though the differences between Azad and Yash Pal were ironed out, Veer Bhadra Tiwari was turned out of the party for disobeying its rules and the factory was also closed.

Besides issues related to the party discipline, one reason for taking this harsh step against Yash Pal was that he got Prakash Vati through elopement. Any step taken by her parents could be extremely harmful to the party. Many members had already harmed the party through their love affairs.

8
He Is Martyred

On one side, sentence to death by hanging had been pronounced in the case of Bhagat Singh, Raj Guru and Sukh Dev, and, on the other, Chandra Shekhar Azad had been declared an absconding criminal. During this period of his being at large, he was moving from one place to another, hoodwinking the police. The police was just after him and many informers were also roaming about in the interest of reward. The police would resort to search on the slightest suspicion. But only one question was uppermost in Azad's mind as to how to strengthen the party. Perhaps, he was thinking of going to South India to achieve this objective.

He reached Allahabad to transform this idea into action. Finally, on 27th February, 1931 that unfortunate day arrived. Azad was seated in Alfred Park along with one of his companions, Sukh Dev Raj. It was 10.00 A.M. Perhaps, a traitor informed the police about his presence in Alfred Park. Just then two police officers, Bisheshar Singh and Dalchand, came there to verify the information. Dal Chand knew Chandra Shekhar Azad. He saw him from a distance and recognised him. After that both of them returned and immediately passed on this information to C.I.D. Superintendent of Police, Nott Baver. Nott Baver immediately reached Alfred Park in his jeep and parked it within 10 yards of where Azad was. He got down from his jeep and advanced towards Azad. He wanted to capture Azad alive, so pointing his revolver at him he asked him to surrender. Well, how could Azad do this? He got up. He replied to Nott's warning by taking out revolver in his hand. Nott Baver fired a short. In reply Azad also fired. The white's shot hit Azad's leg, while Azad's shot hit Nott's shoulder. Then firing started from both the sides. Possibly, more police reinforcement arrived. Nott Baver's wrist was injured. Firing was going on continuously.

But due to wrist injury, Nott Bavir took cover behind a tree.

Azad also dragged himself to take cover behind a tree. He had enough cartridges. Though he was not willing and protested, yet Azad, brushing aside all objections, forced Sukh Dev Raj to run away from the scene. He alone continued raining shots on the policemen. After Nott's taking cover behind a tree, he was replaced by the police officer, Bisheshar Singh. Azad aimed at him and shot through his jaws. Bisheshar Singh had to pay heavy price for this. His jaw could not be set right, and he was relieved of work before retirement.

For quite a while the firing continued from both the sides. It is said that when Azad saw that only one cartridge was left in his revolver, he set it to his temple and pulled the trigger. Azad went into eternal sleep. Even in the process of dying he proved the relevance of his name 'Azad', because he used to say, "I am Azad (independent), and will live like an *azad* person. The police will not be able to capture me alive."

And so it happened. His dead body was lying on the ground. The police stepped forward but for once none dared to touch him. Lion is after all a lion. If he had a little life left in him, he could finish off anybody who touched him. So, before touching his body the policemen fired one shot on his leg. Then they lifted and took him away.

When nearby people came to know that Azad had been surrounded, then a crowd gathered in front of the Muir College, and were shouting the slogan 'Long Live Azad' as they witnessed the incident. The attention of the policemen was drawn towards the slogan-shouting crowd only after Azad fell down on the ground. Then Nott rushed towards them with his revolver. On this, the people ran away towards Muir Central College and the compound of the Muslim Hostel. At this time he was in a hurry to take away the dead body of Azad, so he did not pursue long the slogan-shouting persons and returned. After this the police carried away Azad's body in a lorry, and it was announced that Azad died in police firing.

Different opinions have been expressed with regard to who informed the police about Azad's presence in the Alfred

Park. In some books we find a mention that this information was passed on by Veer Bhadra Tiwari. However, according to some other persons, one *Seth* (a moneyed man) of Allahabad informed the police of his presence there. Shri Manmath Gupta has not directly named Veer Bhadra Tiwari performing the duty of an informer to the police, but his thoughts indicate that this mischief was done by Veer Bhadra. Shri Gupta writes:

"It was 27th February 1931. It was 10.00 O'clock. Chandra Shekhar Azad was strolling on the road from Chowk in Allahabad to Katra, along with Sukh Dev Raj. He was all of a sudden taken aback. The fact is that he saw Veer Bhadra Tiwari. This man, Veer Bhadra Tiwari, was arrested under the Kakori Conspiracy Case, but was released for some mysterious reasons. Since then, members in the party suspected him. But Veer Bhadra was such an experienced and clever man in talking that people were taken in by him. Not only this, he became a prominent member of the party. It is said that his style of conduct was such as both the party and the police treated him as their own man. Azad, in a way, was a very simple man and was very easily taken in by his tricks. After being cheated by him on many occasions, he had finally decided to keep him off. Veer Bhadra also knew that in this way he had been turned out of the party. So when Azad saw Veer Bhadra in Allahabad, he became alert. Azad and Sukh Dev Raj went to Alfred Park and sat at a place. In the meanwhile the police officers, Bisheshar Singh and Dal Chand, came there. Between the two, Dal Chand recognised Azad."

According to Shri Yash Pal Sharma and Shri Yogendra Sharma, the two authors of '*Bharat Ke Teen Krantikari*' (Three Revolutionaries of India), the role of informer was performed by a rich friend of Azad, who held in trust some money of the revolutionary party.

At this time Azad was in Prayag. He had a rich friend. The funds of the revolutionary party were parked with him. Chandra Shekhar Azad was on the look out for re-organising the party. He needed money for this work. He went to his friend, Seth, and demanded money. The Seth had developed some ill-intentions. Since the Seth could not say 'No' to Azad.

he cooked up some ruse and postponed the matter for a day or two. He said that he was likely to receive money in a day or two. He would give it to Azad as soon as he received it. Chandra Shekhar Azad could not sense his ill-intentions as he did not observe any conspicuous difference in his behaviour. Earlier also, he had delayed for one or two days in giving money. Just casually the Seth asked Azad: "Where are you going now Azad? Why don't you stay here with me?"

"No, I am going to Alfred Park now. I have some work there. I'll come tomorrow. Kindly arrange money."

Just as Azad left Seth's house, he informed the police. It was 27th Feb, 1931. The superintendent mobilized the police from the whole city, and ordered it to surround Alfred Park. Chandra Shekar Azad was talking to his companion. He saw the police from a distance. He looked around and found that the police was closing in from all sides like a dark cloud.

Shri Vyathit Hridaya, in his book *Chandra Shekhar Azad*, has combined the two incidents together in the following description:

"Azad's thoughts were drawn to Prayag. He remembered that eight thousand rupees of the revolutionary party were lying with a trader. Why shouldn't I go to Prayag and collect that money from the trader? It would be O.K. that the money of the revolutionary party was utilized for the organization. Then why shouldn't I leave for Prayag right today? I shouldn't delay this work any further. But it would be better to see Tiwari before going to Prayag. In this hour of trouble none else is my own than Tiwari. It would be better I sought his advice. Azad rose as he thought, and set out to see him at his house. He discussed with Tiwari after reaching his house and unfolded his entire plan to him. Then he left for Prayag that night.

"After reaching Prayag, Azad made a small forest near Jhunsi the place of his residence. He bathed daily in Ganga river and lived in the forest in the guise of a *brahmachari*. Staying in the forest, he was trying to get in touch with that trader who owed the party money. Who was that trader? What was his name? We donot find any mention in this context anywhere. What I heard those days, on the basis of that I presume he was not a routine businessman, rather

     Chandra Shekhar Azad : An Immortal Revolutionary of India

he was the owner of a big press, and published two papers. He lived in the guise of a patriot. Revolutionaries like Bhagat Singh and Azad frequently visited his house. When Azad went to Prayag, then on one or two occasions Tiwari also met him in Jhunsi. He had met that press owner as well with whom eight thousand rupees were deposited. Somehow an inspector in C.I.D. came to know of the relations between Azad and Tiwari. The inspector reached Tiwari. Taking him into a net of self interest, he spoke, "I understand you are a close friend of Azad. You know where Azad is these days. You are leading a life of poverty. But if you give me the address of Azad, you can very conveniently get ten thousand rupees of reward."

"Tiwari refused straightaway. He said, "I donot know anything about Azad." Tiwari was a close friend of Azad, but he was not a revolutionary. Azad trusted him a lot. Whenever he came to Kanpur, he always visited him. He knew all the activities of Azad. Where he went? What he did? He knew all this. Though Tiwari had refused, the inspector followed it up seriously. Further reasoning with him, he said, "You will surely not only get rupees ten thousand as a reward, the government will give you a pension as well. Your children and you will lead a comfortable life. You will pass your old age in comfort. Azad is bound to be caught one day or the other. Why do you lose an opportunity so close to you? No one helps others in this world. Wise is one who grabs an opportunity at hand."

The efforts of the inspector ensnared Tiwari's heart in self-interest even though his innermost reaction was one of self-condemnation. The voice of conscience said, "You are indulging in a breach of trust with a friend who trusts you. He is a patriot, a pious soul. You'll get him arrested. You'll not find room even in hell."

"But self-interest overpowered the inner voice of conscience. Tiwari's heart tripped. He told the inspector, "If the total money of reward is passed on to me in advance, I'll give you clues regarding Azad."

The inspector said, "Collect half of money today, right now. The other half will be given when Azad is arrested."

And the inspector placed currency notes of five thousand

rupees before Tiwari. His mouth salivated as he saw the notes. Gulping saliva down his throat he picked up the wad of notes, and blurted out that secret of Azad which nobody knew.

Tremors shook the earth. Mother India's *palloo* was drenched in tears. But there was nobody who understood the value of these tears. Oh! You, the progeny of Jay Chand. It's because of you that the Britishers ruled India, and it's because of you that the freedom and unity of India is endangered. In what words can you be condemned? In what words?

Tiwari was taken to Allahabad. He was introduced to the police there. The police of Allahabad chalked out a plan to arrest Azad with Tiwari's co-operation. Tiwari started working according to that plan. He was weaving dreams.

Tiwari was immersed neck-deep in self-interest. He thought if his face was blackened, why shouldn't he get it pretty darker so that the messengers of hell found it convenient to recognize him. Whatever a man did, he did it fully, and did it pretty well, he concluded.

Tiwari was thoroughly drowned in self-interest now. He reasoned to himself that he was sure to get ten thousand rupees from the police. Why should he not pocket that money also which was lying with the press-wallah. Even if Azad tried hard, he would not be able to make out anything. He trusts me completely. Whatever I report to him, he would take it as true and act accordingly.

Tiwari reached the owner of the press. He said to him: "Azad needs money rather urgently. He has sent me here. Please give me. I will pass on to Azad the eight thousand rupees of the party which are with you."

The owner of the press and Tiwari were known to each other very well. After hearing Tiwari the press-owner said, "I don't have the money with me at present. Can't you persuade Azad to allow me some more time to collect and pay?"

The fact of the matter was that the intentions of the owner of the press had turned malafide. He did not want to part with the money. He thought to himself that the police was shadowing Azad like anything. He was not likely to come to ask for money himself. If someone else came, I would put out ruse and bide time. Then why should I not corner the whole money?

Tiwari said. "You know Azad very well. He does not spare anybody who goes back on his words. It is in your interest that you gave this money to me."

The owner of the press said, "I do not have the total amount. I have only two thousand rupees. If you like I can give you two thousand rupees now."

Tiwari thought of making the best of a bad bargain. He was getting two thousand rupees free. Not a bad idea.

He said, "O.K. Bring two thousand. I will persuade Azad somehow to agree to this."

The owner of the press gave two thousand rupees to Tiwari and thought that it was a good riddance to pay just two thousand against the liability of eight thousand rupees. He could now keep the balance six thousand with him.

Tiwari left with the money. That very day he went to Jhunsi and met Azad. He said to Azad, "I have met and talked to the owner of the press. He is coming sharp at ten in the morning on 23rd February in Company Garden. He will meet you there under the tree opposite library, just close to *nullah* and pass the money on to you."

Azad gave credence to what Tiwari had said. He said, "O.K. I'll reach under that tree before 10.00 o'clock."

The poor Azad did not know that the one whom he trusted was sending him to the jaws of death.

Tiwari returned afer meeting Azad and informed the police about the entire arrangement.

It was 12.00 noon on 23rd March, 1931. The sun was getting hot C.I.D. men were roaming in the Company Garden in plain clothes. As per arrangement with Tiwari. Azad reached Company Garden with one companion before 10.00 o'clock. He sat under the tree next to the *nullah* and waited for the owner of the press.

Just a little time passed when Azad saw the policemen there. He told his companion, "It seems the police knows that I am here. You leave this place before the police closes in on me."

His revolutionary companion did not want to leave Azad, but he forced him to go. He snatched a bicycle from a man nearby and pedalled away.

Shortly after Azad's friend left, Superintendent of Police, Nott Baver, reached there with a posse of policemen. Inspector Bisheshar Singh of the Police Deptt. was with him.

From a distance Nott Baver spoke in a tone of warning, "Surrender, or you will be shot dead."

Azad stood up. He replied to Nott Baver with a shot. The bullet hit his wrist. His wrist bone, though not broken, got punched, and possibly dislocated.

After that the police started firing. Azad took cover behind the tree in self-defence. He replied the police firing with firing.

Azad faced the posse of police with great bravery. Though the policemen were in large numbers, they could not deflect Azad in courage. Unfortunately cartridges came to an end, except one and the last.

Azad set the pistol to his temple and fired the last cartridge. The cartridge shot through his temple, passing out from the other side.

Azad fell into the lap of the earth and died.

In the foreward of his book, Shri Vyathit Hridaya wrote:

"The scene of Azad's sacrifice, which I saw, still floats in front of my eyes. It inspires me, encourages me. I have read again and again about his sacrifice and later I have collected facts. Amar Shaheed Chandra Shekhar Azad is the result of that. I can say that whatever has been written in it has base and facts."

It is clear that Shri Vyathit Hridaya has claimed authenticity of facts in his book. 23rd March, 1931 (or 23rd Feb., 1931) has been mentioned as the day of Azad's martyrdom, whereas the fact is that this is the martyrdom day of Bhagat Singh, Raj Guru and Sukh Dev.

Sukh Dev Raj was with Azad till up to sometime before the last event. According to him, it happened like this:

"On the morning of 27th February, when I started on my

bicycle after breakfast,   met Azad Bhaiya on the way. We moved on to the park, talking. Bhaiya was asking me, since I had been to Burma, if I could tell him whether people could escape from India via Burma. I passed on to him the information I had in this regard. We reached the park talking. There, one person, sitting on the bridge, was cleaning his teeth with datum (a green stick of *neem* or *kikar* used for cleaning teeth). He started looking at Azad closely. Azad suspected something on seeing his eyes. He told me that much. I looked at that man, but he turned his face away.

"Talking, we moved ahead. In the meanwhile a vehicle came and stopped in front of the road. One British officer and two constables in white dress came out of it and, coming near us, asked 'Who are you?' 'What are you doing here?' In the course of talking that officer took out his pistol. On this Bhaiya put his hand to his pistol, and I to mine. Just as the white man started talking as he drew near, both started firing. The white man shot first, Azad later. The white man's shot hit Azad in the leg, Azad's shot hit his shoulder. Firing started from both sides. One shot struck his lung, tearing his right arm in the way. Even then he continued firing. A shot from Azad broke the white man's wrist. He tried to run away in his vehicle to save his life. Azad was all drenched in blood, still he punctured the vehicle's tyre with one shot.

"On this that white man and his men hid themselves behind a tree. Azad also took cover of a tree. Again firing started from both sides. In the meanwhile Azad ordered me to clear out from there. He fell fighting and firing. But he saved the life of one of his compatriots. Azad's dead body was lying on the ground, but none of the policemen dared to go near him. Finally, that white officer asked a policeman to fire at the deadbody from a distance."

Many writers do not consider this version of Sukh Dev as credible. According to many books. Sukh Dev himself was a man from the police. According to Yash Pal, the story of Veer Bhadra Tiwari acting as the police informer was fabricated by Sukh Dev. Suspicion further settles down on Sukh Dev from yet another angle. He was with Azad during this encounter most of the time. How is it he did not suffer a single shot? How could he run away from police safely and unhurt? Is it possible that the police did not deliberately shoot at him?

In this respect the following doubt of Shri Manmath Nath Gupta appears justified:

"According to Yash Pal, the party had been disbanded. The Central Committee had scattered. But this can be asked as to why there was such a gathering of the revolutionaries on that horrible day. Yash Pal was there. Pandey was there. Sukh Dev Raj and Veer Bhadra were there. The question is who betrayed him. There were many who singly or collectively could betray. I remember that one man out of the gathering on the half-century martyr's day of Azad in Allahabad instantly confessed before me that if he opened his mouth you would see many heads rolling."

Whatever the evidence and whatever Yash Pal might say about the double role Veer Bhadra was playing as C.I.D., there were other countless persons who were jealous of the reputation of Bhagat Singh and Azad. They considered Azad as an impediment in their way to success.

Whatever the truth, this much is certain, that Chander Shekhar Azad met his death as he courageously faced and fought the police. These different opinions do not whittle down in any respect his sacrifice and monumental contribution to the history of India's fight for freedom. It is but natural that controversies and various versions are floated in the name of great men.

The police carried away the dead body of Azad. Those who were shouting slogans 'Long Live Azad' went inside the park after this incident. They picked up the soil soaked in Azad's blood and took it home, treating it as final relic, and a sacred, rare legacy. Shri Vyathit Hridaya himself had witnessed this event and had picked up the soil. He wrote:

"When the police left, we went under that tree. We saw, the soil was coloured in blood. We took that soil to our individual homes. That soil remained with me for a long time. But it was soil only. Now it is mixed with other soil and is a part of it."

A sinner is always suspicious. So, the British government feared that, in the event of the dead body of Azad being handed over to the people, they might lose control on their feelings and sentiments. So his dead body was not handed over to the public. Not only this, his death was not announced and his dead body was quickly cremated. Somehow Rajarishi Purushottam Das Tandon and Shrimati Kamla Nehru came to know of his death. They reached the place of cremation with a few other persons. So, they picked up a few pieces of unburnt bones from there, the last residue of this great revolutionary. Two or three days later a meeting was held in which Rajarishi Purushottam Das Tandon and Shrimati Kamla Nehru participated. People offered tributes to their dear late revolutionary. The wife of the famous revolutionary Shachindra Nath Sanyal was also present. Paying her tributes to Azad, Shrimati Sanyal said:

"People have encased the ashes of Khudi Ram Bose in amulets and placed them round the necks of their children so that they could be brave like him. have come to collect a pinch of Azad's ashes in the same spirit."

On this, people applied the ashes of Azad to their forehead. Hardly any ashes were left. They were immersed in Triveni, the confluence of three rivers.

Now the Indian public had only memories of this matchless son of mother India. The park where Azad died fighting bravely became a sacred ground. The tree behind which he took cover and fired at the police became a sacred object, an idol to worship. People started worshipping it, and offered flowers as a mark of their deep respect. But the Britishers could not bear it. They got that tree cut, so that nothing was left behind for people to remember and recognize. But such destruction of physical objects does not take away the memories of the man. Azad lived in the hearts of Indians and will live as long as they live. The death of Azad took away one of the finest brave persons and an honest patriot of India. And with it ended an era of the revolutionary period.

9
Some Inspiring and Memorable Events of Azad's Life

It is better to burn out in a moment of intense flare of light than to burn slowly with a smoke for a long time. Brave Chandra Shekhar Azad exemplified this saying in his life. He carved out an unparalleled place for himself in Indian history just in a brief life span of 25 springs.

In a way the entire life of Chandra Shekhar Azad is an inspiring saga from which his countrymen can learn the sentiments of sacrifice, love for the country and fearlessness. Besides, there are some such motivating events of his life which force a man to sit up and think about him. And people find themselves unconsciously developing a feeling of abiding and deep reverence for this wonderful person who martyred himself for his love of motherland just in the prime of his youth, abjuring all wherewithals of happiness, convenience and indulgences. Many scholarly writers have described these memorable episodes of Azad's life in their books. Some of them are being reproduced here below:

* Once somebody conveyed to Shri Ganesh Shankar Vidyarthi that the parents of Azad were in a very miserable state and did not have anything to eat. Vidyarthiji was deeply pained to learn this. When Azad came to see him, he gave two hundred rupees to Azad with a request to remit them to his parents. Azad took the money but spent it on the activities of the party. When he met Vidyarthiji again, Vidyarthiji asked him if he had sent that money to his parents. On this Azad said, "Vidyarthiji, my parents sometimes do get something by way of food, but there are many young men in my party who have to remain hungry on many occasions. My parents

are old and even if they died it would be no loss to the country. But if a young man of my party died due to hunger, it would be a matter of great shame to us and the country too would be immensely harmed."

* Azad exercised regularly and lived a life of restraint. As a consequence he developed a strong well-formed and attractive body which caused many young girls to be instinctively enamoured of him. We have already written in the context about the affectionate relations developed by Azad in the family of Thakur Malkhan Singh at Dhimarpura. In this family Thakur Malkhan Singh's elder sister also lived whom Azad and his companions addressed as *Jiji* (elder sister). Once a friend of *Jiji* had come to her house to see her. She was mother of quite a few children, yet she carried her youth about her. She was a widow, but she still sought a man with great urgency. She lost her heart to Brahmachariji (Azad). She told her heart's intent to *Jiji*. *Jiji* advised her not to do anything of that sort, but she remained insistent. It was a summer night and Azad was sleeping on the open roof. She came to Azad's bed and sat there. Azad thought that possibly *Jiji* would also be coming. When after waiting for some time *Jiji* did not come, Azad asked her the reason of her coming there. On this the lady smiled and advanced towards Azad. Azad was stepping back as she continued advancing. She threatened Azad that if he did not respond to her advances, she would shout and bring a bad name to him. Seeing no way out of the situation, Azad jumped from the roof and reached the Hanuman temple.

* Azad and his companions lived at the palace of Raja of Khaniadhana. The police got information to this effect. So, the government took control of the state and appointed a person named Prabhu Dayal as its administrator, who kept a watch on the Raja as well. Once the Raja and Prabhu Dayal were sitting in the garden. By chance, Azad also reached there. The Raja was highly surprised to see Azad there in this unexpected manner. As a mark of respect he got up and instantaneously said, "Panditji, you are welcome."

Prabhu Dayal, who was sitting by the Raja, also got up.

The Raja requested Azad to be seated. Just then Prabhu Dayal asked, "who is this Panditji?"

"He is a renowned astrologer", the Raja Saheb said.

Prabhu Dayal wanted to know his name. The Raja Saheb suddenly felt nervous. Azad sensed his nervousness and pat came his reply, "Kishan Lal."

Thus he saved the situation from going out of hand.

* Raj Guru was a man of romantic disposition. Once he got a very good calendar which had the picture of a beautiful woman on it. He hung that calendar on a wall in the factory. Azad saw it, tore it to pieces and threw away. A little while later when Raj Guru saw this plight of the picture, he picked up the pieces and asked, "Who has done this?"

" I did", Azad spoke.

"Why did you tear away this beautiful picture?"

"Because it was beautiful."

"Does this mean that you will destroy whatever is beautiful?"

"Yes, I will."

At that time Azad was angry. A man says many things when he is angry but he does not mean them. This happened with Azad also. In a very short time his anger subsided. After an hour he noticed that Raj Guru was saying something. "We have set out to make the world more beautiful and here all beauty is being destroyed. This is very strange."

On hearing this, Azad's anger also evaporated. He cursed himself. Then with the purpose of assuaging the feelings of Raj Guru he said, "See, I did not mean that I would destroy Taj Mahal. I meant that since we have taken a vow of celibacy, we should restrict ourselves to that at this time. I do not want that we are led astray by beauty at this time."

* Azad himself maintained the accounts of the party funds so that not a single paisa was misused. The members of the party were in Lahore just a few days before Saunders' murder incident. Azad gave every member just four annas per day for food due to paucity of funds. But Bhagat Singh spent that money for seeing a movie, which he received as food allowance. Back from the movie, he informed Azad how he spent that money. Azad shouted at him long and angrily for this. He maintained such wrong addictions were harmful for the

revolutionaries. No member of the party could be permitted for such a thing. Then Bhagat Singh told him that the picture was about the freedom struggle of America. After that Azad gave him another four anna coin and asked him to go and take food first.

* Once Azad was going to some place near clock-tower in Chandni Chowk, Delhi. On the way he was stopped by a few girls who said, "Either serve the country or wear bangles and sit at home."

Azad put his hand forth, and said, "I cannot serve the country. If you feel like it, put bangles on my hand." Then all the girls, one by one, tried to put bangles on his wrist. But none could force bangles on his wrist. Defeated, they said, *Bazar* doesn't have bangles bigger than these. So, fine, go and serve the country."

Smiling Azad moved ahead. The girls were just looking in his direction, hardly knowing that the man they met was Azad.

* Plan had been chalked out to explode the bomb in the Assembly. Bhagat Singh and Batukeshwar Dutt had been selected to do this job. Both of them, Shiv Verma, Jai Dev and other members of the party had been ordered to go out of Delhi. Azad was to go to Jhansi. So Shiv Verma also came to the railway station to see him off. On the way he told Shiv Verma, "Prabhat! Now in a couple of days both of them (Bhagat Singh and Batukeshwar Dutt) will become the country's legacy. Till then treat them as guests and take care of their comfort." (Shiv Verma was addressed as Prabhat in the party).

* In 1921 he was about fifteen years' old when he was sentenced punishment of fifteen cane-lashes. His whole body had been bloodied. As per jail rules, he was given three annas. He threw those three annas on the face of Ganda Singh, jailor, and left.

* Azad was a pure vegetarian since birth. He would go hunting but did not eat meat. Later on, under the influence of Bhagat Singh he had started taking eggs. Bhagwan Das, while narrating an incident of his life, wrote in this context:

"Azad was a strict vegetarian Brahmin in his food habits as per his upbringing and personal grounding. The demon of untouchability in him was exorcised immediately on his working under the leadership of Ram Prasad Bismil. In the role of a leader of H.S.R.A. he did not advance any specious arguments against meat eating, but he did not like it. Hunting he enjoyed but himself did not eat meat. At Raja Saheb Khaniadhana's palace I used to go hunting and openly ate meat as well. He was slightly angry with me for this. Bhagat Singh often teased him through his lecturing on the *Kshatriyas* and the utility, lawfulness and desirability of meal-eating for those who acted like *kshatriyas*. When Azad called me to Lahore at the time of the murder of Saunders, I was amazed to see Azad under the spell of Bhagat Singh. "What is this, Panditji?" I asked. Azad said, 'There is no harm in eating egg. Scientists have called it just like a fruit." That was Bhagat Singh's logic. Azad was just repeating it. As if passing on an information, I said "Perfectly right, Panditji, the egg is a veritable fruit. In that case the hen can be nothing but a tree. I can't be expected to spare it." Bhagat Singh burst into a hearty laugh. In fact, Kailash, you can be an excellent logician. So Panditji, what do you say?" Being mildly and lovingly angry, Azad intercepted, saying, "You bastard! On one hand you are feeding us eggs and on the other you are lecturing as well."

* Once Bhagat Singh asked, "Panditji, tell us about your place of birth and relatives, so that we may assist them in case of something untoward happening to you, and tell our countrymen where this martyr was born."

Expassing a bit of his dislike, Azad said, "You are concerned with me or my relatives? Why do you want to know where I was born or who my parents were? People at my home do not want that somebody assists them, nor do I appreciate that somebody writes my biography. If you talk like this, then what will happen to our oath of secrecy?"

* The reminiscences of Ashfaqullah's brother, in his own words:

"I met Ashfaqullah in his hanging cell. Ashfaqullah asked me if money was required to fight the case? On this I said, 'You are a prisoner—what can you do? But Ashfaqullah said 'O.K. I'll send you money'."

I came back to Shahjahanpur. A week later when I was

taking my food, someone came to see me. I saw that a young man was standing there. I asked, "What's the matter?"

The young man said "Ashfaq has sent some money for you."

Saying this, he passed on a bag of money to me. I asked him, "What is your name?" He said, "I'll tell you everything, but first give me a match-box. I haven't smoked a *bidi* since morning."

I took that bag, entrusted it to my mother, and taking a match-box returned to see the young man. But he had gone, nobody was there. There were two hundred rupees in that bag. I went to Ashfaq a week later and told him everything. On this Ashfaq smiled and said, "He was Chandra Shekhar Azad. There was a reward on his head. So he exercises caution."

* After Ashfaq's hanging, his brother was carrying his dead body in a goods train. On Balamau station a man in suit came into the train and desired to see Ashfaq's face. Ashfaq's brother uncovered the face of the dead body. The man in suit saluted thrice. He saw the face in the light of a lantern. Tears were streaming down his eyes. Then he asked to cover the face of the dead body. Ashfaq's brother asked him his name. On this, the man took the lantern from him and said that he would be back shortly. After this, the man did not return. Ashfaq's brother recognished that he was Azad.

* Sometimes, figuring out the image of his life partner, he would say, "We are moving from one mountain to another. We have two rifles, one on her shoulder and one on mine. We have a bag full of cartridges. She is loading the rifle and I am firing incessantly."

* It is said that once Bhagat Singh and Azad were joking among themselves. The topic was how they would die. Azad said to Bhagat Singh that he (Bhagat Singh) would be arrested from a cinema hall seeing a movie, and die untimely. In reply, Bhagat Singh said it would not be that easy for the police to eliminate Azad, because it would not get rope to hang such a fat neck. One rope would not do. They would have to find two ropes, one for the neck and the other for his

stomach. On this Azad laid his hand on his pistol and said that as long as it was with him, it would be impossible for anybody to arrest him.

* Once some persons advised him that since the revolutionary party was as good as non-existent, he should run away to Russia because if he was caught he was surely going to be hanged. On hearing this Azad said, "Don't talk to me about Russia etc. My body has been made out of Indian soil, I will merge in the dust of this country fighting the enemy for India's freedom."

* Once Azad had come to Lansdown along with his companions—Bhagat Singh, Ram Chandra, Master Chhail Bihari La and Vishwambhar Dayal and was training them in shooting in the hills. In the meanwhile, a few of his companions expressed a desire to see Azad's shot, because he was a deadly shooter, a super marksman. Azad acceded to their wish. His friends asked him to aim at a leaf on the tree. Azad took the aim and fired five shots. But the leaf did not fall. His friends were highly disappointed and thought that he had missed the mark. Finally, that leaf was plucked. It had five holes bored by the five shots. Seeing this, his friends could not help admiring him.

10
Personality and Thought

Chandra Shekhar Azad is an unforgettable, rare and wonderful personality of Indian history. Though Born in a simple and very poor family, Azad played a role in the history of India's fight for freedom, which is thoroughly unique and singular. Any person, who takes into account his family background and his activities, is forced to admit that a graceful individuality as that of Chandra Shekhar Azad is rarely born. Such persons transform themselves into an ideal and leave a message to the coming generations that if a man is competent he makes a place for himself irrespective of his financial position or below-normal family background. A man's individuality is important. It hardly matters what wealth he inherits or what was his family education or age.

Though Chandra Shekhar Azad did not write any book or delivered long lectures to express his thoughts, even then a clear expression of his views and personality is found in the activities of his revolutionary life. One is introduced to the following traits of his life from his activities:

A Self-Made Individual

Chandra Shekhar Azad was born in a very poor family. His father's financial position was so miserable that he was unable to send his son to any school for reading. Describing this poor condition of his family, Bhagwan Das wrote in the context of his party:

"Among Azad's compatriots, i.e. the young men who worked under his leadership, there was hardly anyone who was less educated than him. Hardly anyone was born in a family poorer than his. None other in his family, father, brother or any other relative, had even remotely been endowed with patriotism, sacrifice, intense discipline, courage or any other form of greatness."

Shri Manmath Nath Gupta, in this context, writes:

"His father, Pandit Sita Ram, was a very ordinary servant. So there was hardly any chance of studying English. Azad was sent to Kashi for studying Sanskrit. He was a Brahmin student, so a very ordinary arrangement for his boarding and lodging was made. In Kashi some religious persons ran some hostels and kitchens for students pursuing Sanskrit. Sometimes blankets and jugs (*lotas*) were distributed. Sometimes some money was also given as *dakshina*."

The above lines of the scholars are a clear indication of those circumstances of Azad's family which he had to face in his childhood and schooling period. But Azad proved that as such school education was not everything. A man's in-born ability can not remain hidden irrespective of the fact as to howsoever pitiable might be his family condition, or whether he got education or not. In their absence, too, a man can rise to the highest position on the basis of his abilities and present an ideal to others in front of which the rich and the highly educated person have to bow in respect. Referring to this aspect of Azad's life, Shri Manmath Nath Gupta writes:

"Though Chandra Shekhar was less educated in terms of school or college education he had a rare capacity to capture the essence of books read. Right from the beginning and always, he lived amidst such well-read revolutionaries who, besides being good scholars, were constantly arguing and discussing on principles."

It is evident Azad enjoyed the company of well-educated revolutionaries. Secondly, practical knowledge hardly required formal education. The history of the world is witness to the fact that many great men of the world were un-educated. All the members of his party, in fact, were highly impressed by his practical knowledge. That is why Azad was made the supreme commander of the organization—the new revolutionary party, 'Hindustan Samajwadi Ganatantrik Sena'.

Gaining expertise in and receiving instructions of practical knowledge are two different things. It is not

     Chandra Shekhar Azad : An Immortal Revolutionary of India

incumbent that a well-educated person possesses practical knowledge as well. Virtues such as practical understanding, courage, sentiments of partiotism, morality etc. are in-born traits of an individual. Azad's personality was imbued with these virtues. Dilating on this quality of Azad, Shri Bhagwan Das writes:

"He reached the position of leadership from practical understanding, indomitable courage, knowledge from books, and on top of it all from the loving care and concern for his compatriots and expert leadership in times of difficulties."

Shedding more light on this topic Shri Manmath Nath Gupta writes:

"It is an error that a man learns from intellectual reasoning alone. Other things also affect. A man's background, which spiritual persons would describe as light emanating from it, also affects a man's sense of honesty and faith. For instance, mind or the process of grasping a thing, is deeply affected by beauty, *rasa* (joy in harmony), smell, word and touch."

He became the leader of well-educated revolutionaries due to his practical understanding. Well-educated and intelligent Bhagat Singh also bowed in deep respect to his personality. Azad was, in fact, a gem in rags, a gem that lit up the world in a new light of his own.

Symbol of Strength of Character

Azad was a true patriot. Freedom of the motherland was the only aim before him. He had surrendered all the joys and indulgences of life to realize this aim. He had been a student of Sanskrit. Obviously he would have studied the *Geeta* also. Therefore, he had imbibed this teaching from the *Geeta*: "Contemplation of objects of desire causes affection, affection causes infatuation, infatuation causes anger, anger causes ignorance, ignorance causes loss of memory, loss of memory destroys mind, and with the destruction of mind everything is lost," meaning thereby that it is absolutely necessary to distance oneself from objects of desire to realize one's aims. Therefore, one comes face to face with an admirable strength of character in Azad's life. His character is an ideal. He saw his mother in eve y woman.

In this respect some of his associates in the party had different ideas. Some associates had already put the party to harm on account of their love affairs with women. Therefore, Azad advised his associates to keep away from women. Shri Veerendra writes about his ideally good character:

"The most apparent aspect of Chandra Shekhar Azad's life was his attitude towards women. He always kept himself away from them. He had a very beautiful body of his own. He had built it over years through hard work and exercise. Therefore, once or twice such a situation came to pass that young women tried to ensnare him in their love. But Azad always said that a revolutionary cannot be in love with two things at one time: That he loves his country, or a young girl. If one loved one's country, then this would call for total sacrifice. There is no room at all for any other love in it. A few of his associates had fallen victim to women's love. This harmed his party as well. Azad was never prepared to excuse a person who harmed the party for his love of women. Once he was ready to shoot down one of his associates for this reason. He was never prepared to suffer moral weakness of this kind in any of his associates."

Moral weakness deflects a man from his duty. The duty in his party was not a personal, selfish one. It was a question of the future of the whole country. Therefore, the discharge of such an important duty involved renunciation of indulgences in an essential manner. Keeping all this in view, Azad insisted upon strict, good conduct. For maintaining discipline in the party, the character of the leader of the party had to be the best. This was the first priority—strict discipline and good conduct were its essentials. Earlier mention has been made of an incident when one night he was sleeping at the house of Thakur Malkhan Singh. There a friend of his (Malkhan Singh's) sister came and sat on his bed. In fact, such moments are the testing time of one's character. He was at the zenith of his youth. It is not given to everybody to control oneself. Such a wonderful self-restraint is possible in a man of Azad's stature.

It is a speciality of Indian culture that people are educated to look at women with respect. Azad was comprehensively influenced by Indian culture. Therefore, he treated every woman with respect as an epitome of magnificent character. In this context a dacoity case has been described in an earlier chapter. He had shot at one of the members of his party because he was misbehaving with a girl where they were committing dacoity.

The aim of the revolutionaries was to free their motherland from the chains of slavery. They were not terrorists. The conduct of the above referred member was in violation of the principles of the revolutionaries. Azad could never bear such a misconduct. In the circumstances, when their only aim was to attain freedom for their motherland, to save the members of the party from moral downfall was all the more important duty of its leader. The rules of safety become more strict during the times of difficulty. So, Azad never allowed any relaxation to his members in such matters. The object dearest to his heart was that people concentrated on the activities of the party. He did not want them to discuss love with women. When he heard or overheard any discussion of this sort, he would repeat his retort: "So the same magnetic issue, one who was attracted was drowned."

Not only the topics related to women, he wanted to keep youths away from all kinds of evils. He said, "a revolutionary should keep off women, wine and cigarettes. These three things can bring about a man's downfall any moment."

This did not mean that he hated women. He wanted to give women a place of respect. He expected the same from the members of the party. He was, however, completely opposed to young men who forgot their duties and were just carried away by sentiments.

Amalgam of Tradition and Progressiveness

He was born in a Brahmin family which was not free from traditional stereotypes. Otherwise too, the society at that time represented more stereotypes in comparison to the society today. Azad was, therefore, naturally affected in his early life by the traditional stereotypes as those of casteism, untouchability, food and drinks etc. He had been a student of Sanskrit also, besides this. So that environment also influenced him.

It is not a matter of surprise that Azad, having been born

and educated in a conventional atmosphere was affected in his early life by malpractices of his society. It is practically impossible for a child to remain untouched by his surroundings. Hindu society on one hand is in the grip of malpractices such as untouchability but on the other it has a great bright aspect also. Azad not only picked up the malpractices, he marched ahead with its great liberal aspect also. The fact is that in his subsequent revolutionary life he eliminated the malpractices and clung on to its good and bright aspect.

In his early revolutionary life, he had the good fortune of having revolutionaries like Ram Prasad Bismal as his associates. Prior to this he was an orthodox Brahmin whereas Pandit Bismil was an Arya-Samaji. He was deeply rooted in religio-social liberalism of Arya Samaj. Azad came under his influence and got rid of narrow thinking related to untouchability etc. He realized the uselessness of this mentality.

After that he came in the contact of Bhagat Singh who was influenced by the principles of Karl Marx and the great revolution of Russia, and was dreaming of a future for India based on these principles. After his contact with Bhagat Singh he became the president of 'Hindustan Samajwadi Ganatantrik Sena'. All this brought about a change in his thinking, and he could not remain unaffected by the socialistic principles of Karl Marx.

Thus an orthodox Brahmin Chandra Shekhar Tiwari became first a liberal Arya-Samaji and then a progressive socialist. But the most noteworthy point is that he never left the admirable cultural aspect of his religion. Though earlier his point of view regarding women was definitely a bit illiberal and he opposed their entry into the party, now his attitude was remarkably changed under the influence of revolutionaries, notably Bhagat Singh. Side by side this is also true that he practised celibacy all through his life and was a strong supporter of good character and respect for women. Shri Bhagwan recorded this transformation of Azad in the following words:

"We should remember that Azad was born in an orthodox Brahmin family of a village in a small state of Alirajpur, which, it would be appropriate to say, had the 13th century mentality in respect of women, casteism and untouchability. And graduating from this environment he became the leader of the frontline of Indian revolutionaries of the third decade of 20th century. At the age of 10-12 years in the form of an orthodox Brahmin he ran away to Kashi to study Sanskrit. From there he was swept into the national wave, offered *satyagraha*, was sentenced to cane-lashes and joined the revolutionaries. Under the leadership of immortal martyr Ram Prasad Bismil he soaked in Arya-Samaji thought and realized the futility of untouchability and idol worship. Later on, under Bhagat Singh's impact, he adopted a socialistic, secular point of view, and became the commander-in-chief of 'Hindustan Samajwadi Ganatantrik Sena'. Azad crossed many stages of evolutionary change from those of an orthodox Brahmin child to those of the front-line revolutionary, progressive and young leader in a very short period. In respect of women, Azad continued to remain a committed Brahmachari all through his life. In line with the earlier tradition, Azad initially opposed the entry of women in the party. Later on women worked in the party, and worked very well. It is clear that Azad underwent through all the mentalities between treating 'woman as a mine of hell' to accepting her as active and equal supporting colleague. In his last days, Azad taught with great zeal all the lady members of the party shooting, using gun and taking aim. He encouraged ladies associated with people having sympathy with the party to join the party. He encouraged them in different forms to participate in the revolutionary activities of their husbands and offer them active co-operation. His conduct with women was very simple and sincere. In spite of all this, he was a sworn enemy of a member of the party who was indecently attracted towards women. He could not tolerate any kind of sexual weakness whatsoever on the part of any member. But nothing was dearer to his heart than to see both husband and wife taking part in revolutionary activities".

Not only this, there was a change in his food habits also, consequent upon a change in his thought due to progressive thoughts of Bhagat Singh. Now he had started taking eggs though he was a pure vegetarian Brahmin as per family practice. Narrating an incident of his life in this context Shri Manmath Nath Gupta writes:

"Azad was a vegetarian Brahmin in his food habits as per his personal practice. The demon of untouchability in him had been exorcised when he worked under the leadership of Pandit Ram Prasad Bismil. As a leader of H.S.R.A. though he did not advance any specious logic, personally he did not eat meat. I used to go hunting at the Raja Saheb Khaniadhana's palace, and openly ate meal. On this he was slightly angry with me. Bhagat Singh often teased him through lecture on desirability, utility and ethics of meat eating for Kshatriyas and people acting as Kshatriyas. During the period of Saunders' murder when Azad called me to Lahore, I was amazed to see him under Bhagat Singh's spell, and now Panditji would gulp a raw egg itself breaking it close to his mouth. Surprised, I asked, 'What's this, Panditji?' Azad's reply was, 'There is no harm in egg. Scientists have called it something like a fruit.' This was Bhagat Singh's logic which Azad was repeating."

The above referred incidents make it clear that Azad was naturally influenced by the thought of his associates. Initially he was an orthodox Brahmin, then he came under the influence of Arya Samaj and finally he turned to socialism. He got rid of the obsolete practices picked up from family environment, which is indicative of his progressiveness. But his progressiveness was creative. He never blindly followed the West in the name of progressiveness. He remained glued to good character and the bright aspect of Indian culture. Various incidents provide a clear proof of it. His progressiveness carried alongwith it the liberal values of Indian culture. In this way he supported welfare-oriented progressiveness in consonance with the contemporary expectations. His life offers a wonderful harmony between liberal traditions and progressiveness subserving the interests of the country.

Ideal Leadership

Azad began his revolutionary life under the leadership of Shri Shachindra Nath Sanyal. After the Kakori Kand this party was scattered. He made fresh attempts to organize the party and by chance came in contact with persons like Bhagat Singh and Raj Guru. They all collectively formed 'Hindustan Samajwadi Ganatantrik Sena'. Every member was impressed by the competence of Azad. So he was made the leader of this party—commander-in-chief. His responsibilities increased as a leader of this party. Azad maintained the dignity of this post.

The first duty of the leader is to keep himself in discipline. Keeping this fact in mind Azad always maintained good conduct and discipline and through this presented an ideal to the members of the party. He kept a close tab even on very small matters knowing that they might, if neglected, blow into dangerous problems in future. He was the leader of the party, therefore he maintained the accounts of the party funds to avoid its misuse. The party generally suffered from paucity of funds. So Azad spent even a paisa very carefully. In this context the following lines from Shri Veerendra are particularly notable:

"Azad was always in a state of high alert regarding his expenses. According to his point of view, people gave money to the party thinking that these youths worked whole time for the country and could not undertake any other job. So they get money for their expenses from here and there. It should not be used for any wasteful item. As a leader of the party, he kept money with himself, and himself distributed it to his associates. Today conditions are different. There was a time when—particularly the days when Saunders was murdered in Lahore, or the bomb was lobbed in the Assembly—Azad used to give four annas to each of his associates for food. He had some associates such as Bhagat Singh who were fond of seeing movies. When he asked Azad for money for this, Azad would flatly refuse. He said whatever money they received from public was to be returned through giving blood. It is not desirable that a revolutionary treats himself to the luxury of cinema."

Such an ideal was necessary for a leader in the interest of party discipline. Therefore, he always advised his associates to keep off wine, women and smoking. He himself was completely free from them.

It is a fact that Azad was born in a poor family and he did not receive substantial education. But he had an in-born talent for leadership. Because of this none raised a voice against his leadership in the party, and it continued to function in an ideal manner. Shri Bhagwan Das, a member of his party, praising his able leadership and unravelling its secret wrote:

"Among Azad's associates, i.e. the persons working under his leadership, hardly anyone was less educated than Azad. Hardly anyone was born to poorer parents than his. He did not grow under the patriotism, renunciation, discipline, devotion or the shadow of any other form of greatness of either his father or brother or any other relative. He assumed the post of leadership, as in the case of Bhagat Singh, not on the basis of hollow logic of bookish knowledge, but on the basis of practical understanding, indomitable courage and on top of it all for the sincere care and concern for comforts and convenience of his associates which he displayed by providing leadership in trying times. Azad's success inhered in his quality for etching out a private place for himself for the personal, emotional attachment with his friends and party members than due to any political values. His sincere, loving personal contact with others had made him a revered and endeared leader among his associates. He created such a trust in their hearts that they were prepared to lay down their lives on his mere hint. Regarding acceptance of Azad's leadership in the party there was never any problem or dispute. This, on one side, reflects admiration for Azad, on the other it speaks for his associates' honesty, devotion and humility, though they were in no way less than Azad in education, intelligence, renunciation and their preparedness for sacrifices."

This was the result of Azad's able leadership, in fact, that all his associates were tied in a thread of unity in spite of their being more educated or having come from financially better off families.

No one coronates a lion in the jungle but he becomes its king due to his valour, and is called *mrigendra* (Lord Indra of all deers). In this way Azad became a leader of the revolutionary party on the basis of his competence though he did not have any solid background of family or of any other sort, and added a completely new chapter to the history of revolutionary movement.

A Man of Indomitable Courage

Indomitable courage was a rare characteristic of brave Chandra Shekhar Azad. This trait is reflected in his life all around and all through, from childhood to his martyrdom. There is no single occasion showing him even the least afraid. One can see the traits of this virtue right from his childhood. Lighting all the match-sticks of intense flash light together and caring the least for his burnt hand on Deepawali in his childhood was an early indication of his future life of indomitable courage.

Later on, when he was just fourteen or fifteen years old, his blood boiled when he saw the police atrocities on the satyagrahis picketing shops selling foreign goods. He could not control himself and he struck the head of police sub-inspector by throwing a stone at him. Such a courageous act at such a tender age, and that too under alien rule, was definitely an act of great courage.

His courageous reply to a magistrate, after being caught for that offence, that his name was Azad, his father's name was Freedom, and his home was Jail was not only wholly admirable, it showed an old head on teen-aged shoulders in those uncommonly deep meanings. He did not express fear anywhere between the pronouncement of sentence of fifteen cane-lashes and its execution. And after punishment he threw in the face of the jailor the money he received for it.

Throughout his revolutionary life, the police was always after him but he always acted with courage. Various incidents of his life have been described in earlier chapters. We see that once he went to see his mother. He came to know that the police was following him. He got ready to face the police head on, but Bhagat Singh stopped him. The second time when he went to see his mother and was sleeping there, the police also arrived. He faced the police with bullets this time. When the cartridges were exhausted, he went over roof with his friend and responded to police firing by throwing bricks lying there. His friend was killed, while Azad, jumping from one roof to another, came out of the police dragnet.

After the Kakori *Kand* a police officer was specifically deputed to collect evidence against him. He always followed him. Azad was fed up with this. Then one day, without caring for anything, he confronted him and pointed his revolver to his chest. Seeing this courage of Azad the police officer was stunned. He vowed not to follow Azad again. Azad spared his life.

Many times he came out of the net of the police and secret detectives by getting into disguise. After Bhagat Singh's arrest he had made a plan for his escape from jail, but unfortunately it did not succeed, and in 1929 he attempted to blow up the Viceroy's special. That too did not succeed.

Thus Azad's total life was full of courageous deeds, and finally he met his martyrdom facing police. He was filled with courage to the core. In fact, he was born *Azad*. The fear of death did not touch him even remotely. He was always ready to face death. He said he was always ready to face enemy's bullets. He was independent, *Azad*. In the absence of freedom, he loved death. About his indomitable courage Manmath Nath Gupta writes:

"He was waging an untiring war against imperialism for the last ten years, fighting under unusual conditions, almost adverse conditions. For the last eight years he was following the path of revolution, following it intensely. This unique warrior never stepped back in the face of any kind of difficulty. It was against his temperament. He never shirked. He loved difficulties as swan loved water. He was at large for the last six and a half years, i.e. since 26th September, 1925. After Saunders' murder since 17th September 1928, the noose of hanging was waiting for him. God alone knows as to for how many hangings and deportations he had entitled himself."

Ideal Friend

Though Azad had to deal strictly with the members of the party in the interest of its discipline, his aim was to see that they are not led astray, or miss out their main objective. In fact, the real friend is one who saves his friend from going the way to evil. Behind this strictness was his sincere concern for the wellbeing of his associates. He was always alive to the happiness and convenience of his friends. That is why the members of the party treated him not so much as a leader but as a guardian. In this context, Bhagwan Das writes:

"Azad, as in the case of Bhagat Singh, got the top position of leadership not on the basis of hollow logic of the bookish knowledge, but on the basis of practical understanding, indomitable courage, and on top of it all a loving and sincere care and concern for the happiness and convenience of his associates, displayed through able leadership in difficult times."

The plan for explosion of a bomb in the Assembly was ready. It had been decided that the bombs would be exploded by Bhagat Singh and Batukeshwar Dutt. Azad had to go to Jhansi for some work. He was going to railway station. One member of this party, Shiv Verma, was going with him upto the station to see him off. He said to Shiv Verma, "Prabhat! Now in a few days both of them (Bhagat Singh and Batukeshwar Dutt) would become the legacy of the country. We will be left with their memories only. Till then take care of their comfort, treating them as guests."

These touching words bring another aspect of Azad before us—the picture of a sentimental friend. The great souls may appear very harsh and strong from outside as they have to follow certain social conventions, but they are soft as flowers at heart. This saying is exemplified by our classical character, Chandra Shekhar Azad.

Shri Veerendra has also recorded one incident of his love for friends. This incident relates to a day or two after the bomb explosion in the Assembly. When he saw Bhagat Singh's photo in the newspapers, he kept it before himself and continued looking at it for a long time, and then a stream of tears flowed from his eyes. This was the first time when somebody saw tears in his eyes. But Azad realized that Bhagat Singh has made a huge sacrifice. Now he will not come back, and possibly he may not be able to see him in his life. This thought disturbed him a little bit, and the man who was considered stone-hearted, melted finally. It was not weakness. It was his love for his dear friend."

He presented an example of rare duty to a friend on 27th February, 1931 when fighting bravely against the police he met his martyrdom. Sensing the gravity of the situation, he forced Sukh Dev Raj, much against his wishes, to go away from there and save his life and martyred himself. Sukh Dev Raj himself has written in this regard:

"On this the white man and his companion hid themselves behind a tree. Azad also took cover of a tree. Firing started from both sides. In the meanwhile Azad ordered me to leave. He martyred himself, fighting. But he saved one of his friends."

This example of saving the life of a friend though getting killed himself is an ideal in itself. To expect something like this from common men would be just a piece of imagination.

His attempts to free Ram Prasad Bismil and Bhagat Singh from jail also show his love for friends. Thus, if Chandra Shekhar Azad is a rare revolutionary, a man of indomitable courage, a man endowed with the highest traits of leadership, a symbol of the strength of character and a political thinker of progressive ideas on one hand, he comes before us as an ideal friend on the other hand.

Synonymous with Patriotism

The whole life of Chandra Shekhar Azad is replete with the feelings of love for his country. Possibly the seeds of this feeling were sown in his heart when he came to Benares from Bhabhra to study Sanskrit. This was a period of political turmoil in India. Events such as the boycott of Simon Commission, Jalianwala Kand took place during this period. These events helped in the sprouting of seeds of love for the country in Azad's heart. His love for the country was first seen in 1921 when the police rained *lathis* on the *sayagrahis* when they were picketing shops which sold foreign goods. Azad could not bear these atrocities and he hit a police sub-inspector with stone.

After this Azad was completely immersed in his love for the country. He gave up his home, his studies—everything for the love of his country. The intoxication for the country brought him in touch with the revolutionaries and then in 1921, after the end of Non-co-operation Movement he became a member of 'Hindustan Republican Association', a revolutionary organization. From here the little plant (of the love for his country) sprouted, developed foliage and got an opportunity to grow into a huge tree.

Now he had only one object before him—to free his country from the clutches of foreigners. Whatever he did, whether it was a dacoity, thuggery, violence or the orgnaisation of the revolutionary organization, he did with this object in mind.

He renounced all the pleasures of life to realize this objective, and welcomed all sufferings for this. He considered all the pleasures of life an impediment in the realization of this objective. Therefore he advised other members of the party to keep away from them. His declaration was clear:

"If one loves one's country, then he will have to sacrifice everything for this. It does not offer any room for any other form of love."

"This declaration of total sacrifice for the love of one's country was not a principlistic aspect of his life, but an action-oriented conduct. We can take one incident of his life as an example. Ganesh Shankar Vidyarthi had given him two hundred rupees so that he could remit them to his parents because they were reduced to such a miserable condition that they were starving. But Azad spent that money on members of his party. When Vidyarthiji asked him, "Have you sent that money home?" Azad replied: "My parents occasionally do get something for eating but there are many young men in my party, who have to remain completely hungry many times. My parents are old. The country will not be harmed if they die, but it will be a matter of great shame if some young man of my party dies in the throes of hunger. Additionally, it will harm the country immensely."

No other thing can demonstrate in a better way his love for the country than this rare and unprecedented sacrifice. Finally, he proved the truth of his word by giving away everything he had, by sacrificing his life. In fact, Chandra Shekhar Azad has become a synonym for the love of the country, synonymous with patriotism.

NEW PUBLICATIONS

Biswaroop Roy Chowdhury
Dynamic Memory Computer
Course **(Updated & Revised)**

Dr. Ujjwal Patni
Power Thinking

Namita Jain
How to Lose the last
5 Kilos

Tarun Engineer
Aim High For Bigger Win

Joginder Singh
Mind Positive Life Positive

Yaggya Dutt Sharma
**The Lord of New Hopes
Akhilesh Yadav....**

Ashu Dutt
Master the Stock Market

Ashu Dutt
Stop Losing Start Winning

Renu Saran
101 Hit Films of Indian Cinema

Renu Saran
History of Indian Cinema

O.P. Jha
**Shirdi Sai Baba: Life Philosophy
and Devotion**

Dr. Sunil Vaid
Why Does My Child Misbehave

Biswaroop Roy Chowdhury
India Book of Records

Biswaroop Roy Chowdhury
Heal Without Pill

Surya Sinha
Perfect Mantras For Succeeding
in Network Marketing

OSHO
The Osho Upanishad

OSHO
Sermons in Stones

OSHO
Tantric Transformation

Subhash Lakhotia
Golden Key to Become
Super Rich

Subhash Lakhotia
Your Money My Advice